THE CLUB MEMBER'S HANDBOOK

THE
CLUB MEMBER'S
HANDBOOK

By

LUCY R. MILLIGAN
*President of the National
Council of Women*

and

HAROLD V. MILLIGAN
*Formerly President of the National
Association of Organists*

THE NEW HOME LIBRARY

New York

An original publication of THE NEW HOME LIBRARY, SEPTEMBER, 1942

THE NEW HOME LIBRARY, 14 West Forty-ninth Street
New York, N. Y.

CL
PRINTED IN THE UNITED STATES OF AMERICA

Foreword

THE URGE to get together, to form a group, may be said to be almost a basic human instinct. All human life, from the most primitive savage community to the most sophisticated civilization, falls back upon this basic ability to organize and to work and play together.

The boy or girl who has never belonged to a club or secret society has missed not only a lot of fun but a lot of valuable experience as well. It may seem a far cry from the gang of little boys who meet in your attic or barn to the Congress of the United States, but in essence the impulse and the process are one and the same. Many future leaders of political and social life are getting their first experience in team work and leadership in the "Our Gang" groups that all children love.

In our clubs we learn self-government, we develop leadership, we handle easily the tools of parliamentary law—(the very word "parliamentary" is significant of the importance of proper procedure)—we clarify and intensify our ideals and put them to work.

Even clubs primarily for pleasure and sociability have their usefulness and tend to strengthen that basic structure of our communal life. The pleasure club, the culture club, the working club—all have certain fundamental principles and follow certain fundamental patterns.

Men have had their clubs for centuries, but the women's club has only recently celebrated its fiftieth anniversary. Today in the United States there are millions of club women and thousands of clubs. Some women's clubs were founded for definite purposes, but most of them were originally groups of women who met together informally for the pleasure of each other's society and for the purpose of studying literature or art or music. A little group of intimate friends got together more or less regularly and the most important items on the agenda were papers about authors and artists and musicians, prepared from the available material in the public library and read by one of the members, and (perhaps even more important) the "refreshments." These "culture clubs" still continue and during the past half-century they have contributed as much to the cultural and intellectual development of America as any one thing, for they represent culture, not dispensed from above, but growing up from "grass-roots."

The culture club soon began to rival the church and the school as a center of community life. The subjects studied expanded in scope and began to include politics, international affairs, local affairs, economic and social problems of magnitude.

Today there are culture clubs and service clubs and (perhaps the ideal group) clubs which combine the two phases. In addition to clubs for men and clubs for women, there are clubs and organizations where men and women meet together.

The rules and practices discussed in this book apply equally to men's clubs and women's clubs. However, since the book will very possibly be of special interest to women readers, we have referred to women in discussing club officers and members. There is a chapter at the end devoted entirely to men's clubs, and at certain points in other chapters mention of men's clubs will be found.

The Club Member's Handbook touches every phase of club

life. If you are a new club member, the book will help you to understand how clubs function. If you have been a member for a number of years, and would like to take a more active part in the work of your club, you will find practical advice which will aid you in preparing yourself for the club activity in which you are especially interested. We hope that whether you are a new or an experienced club member, you will find that this book encourages you to share more fully in the privileges and duties, and increases the satisfaction and enjoyment which comes to you from club life.

L. R. M.

H. V. M.

Contents

FOREWORD v

I HOW CLUBS ARE ORGANIZED
Why Rules of Procedure Are Necessary . . . 1
Fundamental Rules of Procedure 4
When to Rise at Meetings 5
When and How to Speak at Meetings . . . 6
Responsibilities of Officers and Members . . . 7

II HOW MEETINGS ARE CONDUCTED
Calling the Meeting to Order 12
Quorum 12
Reading the Minutes 13
Reading Club Correspondence 14
Treasurer's Report 15
Reports of Committees 15
Corrections in Committee Reports 17
Special Committees 17
Unfinished Business 19
New Business 19
When and How to Adjourn 20
Proper Parliamentary Conduct 22
Wording of Motions 24
Methods of Voting 24
The Presiding Officer 25

III   CONSTITUTION AND BY-LAWS

The Purpose of Constitution and By-Laws . . 27
Outline of Constitution 28
     Name; Purpose; Membership; Officers; Executive Board; Meetings; Amendment
Outline of By-Laws 33
     Membership; Dues; Duties of Officers; Executive Board; Committees; Quorum; Order of Business; Parliamentary Authority; Amendment
Method of Adoption of Constitution 43
Method of Adoption of By-Laws 45

IV   DUTIES AND QUALIFICATIONS OF
     OFFICERS

President 48
Vice-President 53
Recording Secretary 54
Corresponding Secretary 56
Treasurer 57
Executive Board 58

V   HOW MOTIONS ARE MADE AND AMENDED

Making a Motion 60
Seconding a Motion 61
Types of Motions 62
Main Motions 62
Secondary Motions 64
Subsidiary Motions 64
Privileged Motions 67
Incidental Motions 69
Amendments 71
Control of Debate 73
"Out of Order" 74

VI HOW RESOLUTIONS ARE MADE

    Types of Resolutions 75
    Form of Resolutions 76
    Duties of the Resolutions Committee 77
    Submitting Resolutions to the Club 79
    Safeguarding Resolutions 81
    Importance of Resolutions 82
    Publicity for Resolutions 83

VII HOW MINUTES ARE KEPT

    Necessary Materials 84
    What to Include and What to Omit 86
    Minutes of Committee Meetings 87
    For the Permanent Record 88
    Essentials of Correct Minutes 88
    Example of Correct Minutes 90

VIII HOW VOTES ARE TAKEN AND COUNTED

    Terms Used in Connection with Voting . . . 93
        Plurality; Majority; Two-thirds
    Methods of Voting 95
        Acquiescence; Viva Voce; Show of Hands;
        Rising; Roll Call; Ballot; Proxy; Mail; Casting
        One Ballot
    When the Presiding Officer May Vote 102

IX HOW ELECTIONS ARE CONDUCTED

    Methods of Nomination and Election 104
        From the Floor; By Committee; Rotation
    After the Election 113

X HOW FINANCES ARE HANDLED

    Treasurer and Finance Committee 114
    Necessary Equipment for Treasurer's Work . . 115
    Bank Account 117

Bills and Receipts 117
Treasurer's Report 118
Special Funds 119
Correct Signature 119
Legal Receipt 119
Audit 119
Budget 121
    Sources of Income; Dues; Assessments; Money-
    Raising Projects; Total Anticipated Income;
    Anticipated Expenses

XI HOW COMMITTEES WORK
Types of Committees 130
Standing Committees 132
Special Committees 133
Size of Committees 134
Selection of Committee Members 135
Rules for Committee Action 137
Reports by Committees 138
Committee of the Whole 141

XII HOW CORRESPONDENCE IS CONDUCTED
Necessary Equipment 142
Conducting Club Correspondence 144
Good Form in Club Correspondence 146
General Suggestions Concerning Correspondence 148

XIII HOW PROGRAMS ARE CONDUCTED
Selection of Program Committee 150
Powers and Responsibilities of Program Com-
    mittee 151
Subjects for Programs 153
    Study of Current Events
Speakers 155
    Paid Versus Unpaid Speakers; Meeting the
    Out-of-Town Guest

Participation of Members in Programs . . . 161
Methods of Discussion 162
   Debate; Forum; Panel; Round Table; Symposium; Seminar
Club Programs on the Radio 165
The Club Year Book 166
Club Programs in General 167

XIV HOW PAPERS ARE PREPARED

Papers by Members 169
   Older Type of Paper; Influence of Radio on Style of Club Papers; Every Member Must Participate
When Your Turn Comes 173
How to Collect the Material 173
   The Public Library; Magazines and Newspapers; State Libraries; Federal Publications; Other Sources of Information
How to Use the Material 178
Getting It Down in Black and White 180
How Long Should Your Paper Be? 183
Essentials of Presentation 184

XV HOW TO SPEAK IN PUBLIC

The First Attempt 186
Characteristics of a Good Speech 188
How and What to Practice 189
   Reading Aloud; Enunciation; Gestures
Standing Before the Audience 192
   Self-Confidence; Hands and Eyes
Developing Skill Through Daily Conversation . 197
Progress in Public Speaking 198

XVI HOW TO GET THE RIGHT PUBLICITY

Value of Good Publicity 200

The Work of the Publicity Chairman . . . 201
    What Is News?; The Use of Pictures; Contact
    With Editors and Reporters
How to Prepare Copy 207
Co-operation of Officers and Members in Handling
    Publicity 209

XVII THE COMMUNITY SERVICE CLUB
Choosing the Club Activities 211
The Chief Club Projects 213
    Libraries; Community Improvement; Student
    Loan-Funds; American Citizenship; Education;
    International Relations; The Arts: Music,
    Literature, Painting and Other Arts; Other
    Club Projects

XVIII NEW CLUBS FOR OLD
Changing from One Existing Club to Another . 221
Giving New Vitality to an Old Club 222
Organizing a New Club 224
    The First Informal Meeting; The Organization
    Meeting; The Temporary Officers; The First
    Committees; Setting Up a Permanent Organ-
    ization; Planning the New Club's Future

XIX FEDERATIONS OF CLUBS
National Organizations for Women 236
National Organizations for Men 237
Groups for Men and Women 238

XX CONVENTIONS OF FEDERATED CLUBS
Preliminary Plans for a Convention 240
Selection and Duties of Delegates 240
The Necessary Organization and Management . 242

Committees for Conventions 243
Committee on Arrangements; Committee on
Program; Committee on Credentials and
Registration; Committee on Transportation;
Committee on Hospitality; Committee on Ex-
hibits; Committee on Publicity; Committee on
Information
Sub-Committees 247
Decorations; Finances; Luncheons and Dinners;
Ushers and Pages; Music; Conferences; Minor
Details
The Convention Program 248

XXI THE CLUB HOUSE
Advantages 250
Difficulties 251
Club Houses in Small Towns and Rural Districts 251
The City Club 252
Essentials of a Good Club House 253
Financial Problems 255

XXII CUSTOMS AND ETIQUETTE IN WOMEN'S
     CLUBS
Community Activities 257
The Social Element 259
Clothes

XXIII CUSTOMS IN MEN'S CLUBS
The Private and Exclusive Club 262
The Informal Lunch or Dinner Club 263
Programs of Dinner Clubs 265
Hobby Clubs 267
Clubs Interested in Public Affairs 268
The Service Clubs 268
Rotary International; Kiwanis; The Lions

Clubs for Both Men and Women 270
    The National Grange; Parents and Teachers
    Associations; Local Service Clubs

APPENDIX

Glossary of Parliamentary Terms 271
Summary of Parliamentary Law 277
Example of Form for a Constitution 283
Suggestions for Organization of Local Councils 285
National Organizations for Women 287
National Organizations for Men 288
National Organizations for Men and Women . 290
Sources of Information for Club Study . . . 290

INDEX 297

THE CLUB MEMBER'S HANDBOOK

How Clubs Are Organized

WHEN you first attend a meeting of any club or organization at which business is conducted, you will hear words and phrases which may be unfamiliar to you, and you will notice that a rather set program is followed. The procedure may seem complicated and stilted to you, or things may happen so rapidly that you do not quite understand what is being done or how it is being done.

Motions are made and seconded; reports and resolutions presented and disposed of; somebody says something about a "point of order"; there is a lot of talk about an amendment; the presiding officer says abruptly, "Those in favor say Aye, those opposed No, the motion is carried," but as far as you could tell, nobody said either Aye or No. Members of the club seem to know when to stand up and when to sit down; the President and Secretary and various other people speak glibly in what seems to you almost a foreign language or a jargon which you only half understand. As a bewildered outsider, you may feel as if you were watching experts play a game of which you were ignorant.

Why Rules of Procedure Are Necessary

What is this game called "parliamentary law"? Who is to say what is right and what isn't? Why not say just what you mean in plain English and let it go at that? Why have any organization at all, with officers and minutes and reports and what not?

But all these things didn't happen by chance. A club transacts its business according to methods which have been in use for many years, some of them for centuries.

A club, after all, is merely a group of individuals banded together for a common purpose. The methods used by clubs for transacting business are basically the same methods that are used by all groups which work together in meetings and govern themselves. What seems at first to be an affectation or a stilted formula turns out on closer study to be a necessary and direct way of handling the problems which are bound to come up in any assemblage of people, and a sure and definite method of accomplishing the wishes of the majority.

Though you may feel like an outsider at first, there is no reason why you should remain so. You may cherish no ambitions to be President of the club, or Secretary, or even chairman of a committee. You may be quite content to remain just a member of the group, but in order to be a real member and not merely a spectator, it is necessary for you to have some insight into the methods used at meetings, and to know something about the duties and responsibilities of the officers. There is an element of "give-and-take" in all democratic institutions and the presiding officer must depend to some extent upon your understanding and co-operation as a member of the assembly, just as you must depend upon his knowledge and skill in parliamentary procedure. The other officers and chairmen of committees can accomplish their work properly only if you as a member know what they are called upon to do. You, as a member, are the final judge of the success or failure of their efforts, and this requires from you more than a vague and perfunctory impression as to what it is all about.

So do not think that you can sit in an obscure corner and say nothing and still be a worth-while member of the club—worth while either to the club or to yourself. By following understandingly the methods by which meetings are conducted you may be unconsciously preparing yourself to carry greater responsibilities some day, even though for the present you do not take any more active part in the proceedings than to say "Aye" and "No" at the proper times.

Whatever the purpose of the group or club, some form of organization is almost inevitable. There must be some guidance for discussion as well as action; and guidance requires a Chairman, or Moderator, or President. In order to avoid confusion and to achieve some continuity, a record of the sayings and doings of each meeting must be kept, and that means a Recording Secretary. Perhaps some letters must be written, and that means a Corresponding Secretary. And there is almost certain to be a small amount of money involved, perhaps only for postage and stationery, or for luncheons and dinners, but the club needs a Treasurer. And a Treasurer almost certainly calls for an Auditor;—and so it goes. The responsibilities and duties of these officers must be outlined and the limitations of their activities defined, and that means a Charter or Constitution, and By-laws.

Officers and By-laws are not mere formalities or decorations. They are necessary parts of any efficient group action. Their functions and duties are the outgrowth of centuries of experience and experiment. Each club does not have to do its own experimenting, at least in establishing the fundamental machinery of its group activities. This has become standardized. It is necessary that you should know and clearly understand the guiding principles which have been proved by actual experience to be the best.

Fundamental Rules of Procedure

You will find certain fundamental similarities in practically all public meetings for the transaction of any kind of business. There will be at least two members of the group[1] who will be regarded as officials of the meeting, the presiding officer and the secretary. It is possible (though not advisable) to hold a meeting without a secretary; but a presiding officer is absolutely necessary. It makes no difference whether the presiding officer stands upon a stage or rostrum, or behind a table or desk, or merely stands upon her feet in front of the assembly,—she is the central point around which the meeting moves. She must open the meeting, guide its deliberations, and bring it to an end. The secretary is almost as necessary as the presiding officer, for without a secretary there is no official record of what is said and done. Like the presiding officer, the secretary usually occupies a prominent place in the room where the meeting takes place; this is a matter of convenience and efficiency as the secretary must be able to hear what is said and done and must be able to communicate quickly with the presiding officer.

In addition to the table, desk, or rostrum behind which the presiding officer stands, and the papers which the secretary handles as part of her work, another item of physical equipment which may be found in the room where the meeting takes place is a small wooden mallet or hammer which is placed on the presiding officer's table. This is called a gavel, and while it is a small and inoffensive-looking object, it has been, since time immemorial, the symbol of authority, of law and order. A stroke of the gavel by the presiding officer has more power over deliberative and legislative assemblies than a regiment

[1]As mentioned in the Foreword, our examples refer to women's clubs, although the rules and practices described apply to men's clubs also

of soldiers. It typifies our ability to govern ourselves, to make and abide by our own rules of procedure.

When the hour designated for the meeting has come and the group has assembled, the presiding officer stands at the table (or desk or whatever has been arranged for), strikes the gavel once or twice on the table, and says, "The meeting will come to order."

"Coming to order" simply means that those present take their seats, bring their private conversations to an end as quickly as possible, and give their attention to the speaker and to the business which is to follow. Of course, if this does not happen at once, if the group does not show a disposition to quiet down, the presiding officer need not hesitate to use the gavel again and to make the request for order more imperative. At any time during the meeting, the gavel may be used again in calling for order. Sometimes in the course of the discussion of some controversial question, members of the assembly may forget themselves and begin to talk and argue among themselves, instead of paying close attention to the remarks of those who are authorized to speak. A good presiding officer will always keep the meeting in order, and the discussions and debates must always be carried on in the hearing of the entire assembly and never as private conversations.

More detailed description and analysis of correct parliamentary procedure will be found in later chapters. For the moment, we are considering only the characteristics of a club meeting which might puzzle a newcomer not used to the customs and traditions of such assemblies.

When to Rise at Meetings

One question which sometimes embarrasses inexperienced club members is when to rise and when not to rise.

When a meeting is called to order, all present should be seated except the presiding officer. The secretary should be seated at a table, beside the president, or chairman. The presiding officer need not remain standing throughout the entire meeting, but she should stand while addressing the meeting, making announcements, conducting a debate or discussion, calling for nominations, conducting an election, and announcing the result of an election. During the reading of reports, long speeches, and other routine business, the presiding officer may (and should) remain seated.

Any member of the assembly making a nomination, presenting a resolution, making a speech, asking a question or otherwise taking any momentarily prominent part in the proceedings, should rise, but should not remain standing longer than necessary. It is always awkward and sometimes unpleasant to have two or more members of the assembly on their feet at the same time, especially if the chairman is also standing. If two or more rise at approximately the same time, the chairman must decide which one has the right to speak first. She does that by mentioning the name of the one who is to speak, or by nodding in her direction. The presiding officer may emphasize the point by saying, "Mrs. Smith has the floor." The other speakers will then, of course, sit down and await their turn. Mrs. Smith "has the floor" until she has finished what she wanted to say. Any interruptions or questions may be allowed only by permission of the chairman, and the questioner should be permitted to stand only while putting the question. The right to "hold the floor" is a very important one, and should be guarded jealously but not imposed upon.

When and How to Speak at Meetings

Another question which embarrasses untrained speakers is when to use the first person and when the third. It is really very simple. The chairman is commonly referred to as "The Chair," and is addressed in men's clubs as "Mr. President," or "Mr. Chairman," and in women's clubs as "Madam President," or "Madam Chairman." Never speak to a presiding officer as "you."

The presiding officer in turn never says, "I." All statements in his or her official capacity are in the third person. "The Chair recognizes" "The Chair appoints," or "The Chair will consider a motion."

No one may speak in the meeting without first securing permission or recognition from the presiding officer.

Responsibilities of Officers and Members

In addition to the officers (presiding officer, secretary, treasurer), two other essentials in the structure of the club organization are : (1) Constitution and By-laws, and (2) committees.

Constitution and By-laws, like adherence to established rules of parliamentary procedure, are to be regarded as a means to an end, and not as an end in themselves. The great purpose of all rules and forms for organized groups is to serve the will of the assembly and not to obstruct it, to facilitate and not restrain the expression of a group opinion and the accomplishment of a common purpose. What is wanted is a maximum of efficiency and a minimum of misunderstanding. If you will keep this principle in mind, you will find answers to many questions which will come to you while you are familiarizing yourself with the conduct of club meetings.

It is not always practical in a public meeting to discuss all the questions which may arise. Frequently it is necessary to secure more accurate and complete information in regard to the subject at issue. This foundation work must be done in committees and the result brought to the club at a later meeting. At this later meeting the club has a right to a full and frank discussion and may accept, amend, or reject the work of the committees.

You may feel that these formalities,—Constitution and By-laws, reports of committees, parliamentary rules,—are out of place in a small friendly group who have met together for a common purpose and with mutual good will and helpfulness. But no matter how friendly and intimate the group, do not think that methods and order can be entirely dispensed with. Parliamentary law (the term which describes standard rules for all meetings and assemblies) is something which has grown up over the centuries and has been handed down to us by our forebears in its present form as a result of long years of experiment and experience. It has been formulated not to make things difficult, but to make them easy and to prevent misunderstandings. Do not be afraid of parliamentary law. Do not hesitate to make use of it. When you have mastered it, it will be your servant.

When there are a number of members in any club who are inexperienced in public affairs, it is a good idea to gather them together for an hour or two of study of the basic principles of parliamentary law.[2]

If you feel that you are perhaps the only inexperienced member in the group, you may learn a great deal by asking questions, and among other things you may learn that some of your fellow members are just as ignorant of parliamentary usage as you are, and here you may do a little missionary work and organize a study group for mutual benefit.

For the successful conduct of a meeting and for the accomplishment of a common purpose, more is necessary than just a

[2]When a book, devoted entirely to Parliamentary Law, is desired for study purposes, we recommend Robert's *Parliamentary Practice.* As a standard and complete work for reference rather than study, Robert's *Rules of Order, Revised* is recommended.

capable presiding officer and a good secretary. Certain responsibilities devolve upon the members also. A meeting where the members sit silent and bewildered during the business session cannot be expected to accomplish much. When the chairman asks for an expression of opinion on any question submitted to the assembly and receives only embarrassed silence in return, the whole purpose of the assembly is in danger of defeat. For the presiding officer to cope with too many and too long harangues on a pending motion requires firmness and tact, but to cope with blank and unresponsive silence is, if anything, even more difficult. In such cases, if the President has heard expressions of valuable opinion from individuals in the course of private conversations, she may call upon such individuals to express in public what they have already said in private. Once the ice has been broken others will follow and soon the question at issue will be receiving a full and frank discussion.

The members of the club should never be allowed to forget that it is their club and that they have not only rights but also duties. To sit silent during a debate and then afterwards to express disapproval and resentment at the action taken is not to be a loyal club member. On the other hand, to feel too obscure and useless to take part in the discussions of the assembly is not to be a very helpful and co-operative member either. The rights and duties of the members of the group, as regards one another, are founded on and derived from the principle of their absolute equality among themselves. Every member, however humble she may be, has the same right as every other member to submit propositions to the assembly, to explain and recommend them in discussion, and to have them examined and decided upon by the assembly. On the other hand, it is the duty of every member not to obstruct any other member in the enjoyment of equal rights.

It may be said that parliamentary law and all transactions of business in public assembly are founded upon two basic principles,—(1) the absolute equality of all members of the assembly as regards the deliberations and actions of the assembly, and (2) the absolute impartiality of the presiding officer.

How Meetings Are Conducted

THE purpose of this chapter is to outline a simple and typical meeting. We will assume for the moment that no complicated questions of parliamentary law will come up and that a rudimentary knowledge of proper procedure on the part of the presiding officer and others involved will be all that is needed to conduct the meeting and to accomplish what is desired.[1]

The By-laws of the club prescribe an Order of Business, by which the various matters which come before the club shall be taken up, each in turn, and this prescribed order should be strictly adhered to. If at any time this prescribed Order of Business is not followed, any member of the club may call attention to that fact, and the proper order must be attended to.

In addition to the prescribed Order of Business, the presiding officer will also have for her own use a list of matters to be brought up at the meeting. This is called the "Agenda," and it is a personal memorandum for the presiding officer, or the secretary, or one or two other important officers. It is not official, and it is not the Order of Business.

A wise presiding officer will discuss informally with a few people the proposals and projects which may be expected to come up at any meeting, and will plan in advance, as far as

---

[1]In the Appendix, a comprehensive summary of parliamentary procedure is included for those who desire a more complete knowledge of the subject.

possible, just how the making and passing of motions should be accomplished and other necessary actions taken. This is not done with any idea of dictating to the assembly just how it shall act, but merely in the interests of smooth-running efficiency, and for the avoidance of unnecessary delay and confusion.

Calling the Meeting to Order

When the presiding officer stands at the rostrum or table, raps sharply once or twice with the gavel, and says, "The meeting will please come to order," the secretary takes her place at the table or desk beside the presiding officer, and the assembled members take their seats, and all conversation ceases.

Quorum

Practically all clubs provide in their By-laws that a certain proportion of the membership must be present in order to constitute a proper meeting and transact any business. For instance, a club with a membership of approximately 45 may specify that 25 members must be present in order to make any business legal. This required number of members is called a "quorum." Ordinarily it may be assumed that a quorum is present when the chairman calls the meeting to order. If there is any question as to whether or not a quorum is present, a roll-call may be demanded. If a quorum is present, the meeting proceeds as usual. If no quorum is present, no business can be acted upon, although informal discussion may be indulged in by the members present. If only two or three members are lacking in order to make up a quorum, it is sometimes possible to bring them in by means of telephone calls, or by merely waiting for them. A second roll-call is then taken, and if the required number is present, the meeting gets under way. It is important to watch this matter of quorum, as considerable trouble can arise as a result of ignoring it. As a quorum is usually present, one seldom hears the demand for a roll-call in the average club, and if a club experiences difficulty in obtaining a quorum for many of its meetings, it would seem that the estimated quorum is too high and the best thing to do is to alter the By-law and provide for legal meetings with a smaller number of members constituting the required quorum.

Reading the Minutes

When quiet and attention have been established, the Chairman says, "The Secretary will read the minutes of the last meeting."

The Chairman then sits down and the Secretary rises, faces the assembly, and reads the minutes clearly and distinctly.

At the close of the reading, the Secretary sits down, the Chairman rises and says, "You have heard the minutes. Are there any corrections or additions?"

If any member has failed to hear or understand any paragraph of the minutes, she may ask to have them re-read. If anything has been omitted, or if there is any ambiguity in the wording of the minutes, any member may rise and make inquiry or suggestion. Additions or corrections of the minutes need not be put to vote. If your Secretary is capable and conscientious the minutes will be correct as read and need no correction. If, however, an addition or a correction is to be made, the person offering it, rising, says, "Madam Chairman, I suggest that the wording be changed to read,—so-and-so," or "Madam Chairman, I think there is an omission in the minutes." The Chairman, informally, secures the approval of the group, and the Secretary makes the corrections.

The Chairman then says, "If there are no further changes, the minutes will be approved as corrected," and after a brief pause, says "They are so approved."

If there have been no corrections or changes, the Chairman says, "The minutes stand approved as read."

You will sometimes hear a motion to "approve the Secretary's report as read," but this is unnecessarily formal. The statement of the Chairman that the minutes are approved if nothing is heard from the assembly to the contrary is quite sufficient. If a motion to approve is made, however, it must be seconded and voted upon in the usual manner.

If the minutes are approved, and later on, either at the same meeting or at a later meeting, it is discovered that a mistake has been made in them, or something has been omitted, it will be necessary to make a special motion that they be corrected, and a vote must be taken.

Reading Club Correspondence

After the approval of the minutes, the Corresponding Secretary reads all communications which have been received addressed to the club, whether acknowledgements, invitations, or appeals. It is not necessary to accept this report from the Corresponding Secretary unless the club wishes to acknowledge the receipt of a communication, accept or decline an invitation, or otherwise take action on any of the letters read. In that case, a member says, for example, "I move that the Corresponding Secretary be authorized to accept (or decline with thanks) the invitation received from the School Board." Sometimes it is the President who is instructed to reply, as a letter from her may be considered to carry more prestige. Aside from the mere reading of the communications, any action taken must be specifically stated in the motion as made, seconded and passed.

In small clubs, having only one Secretary who combines the

work of both recording and corresponding, the two functions should be treated separately at any meeting, that is to say the minutes read, corrected, and approved before any correspondence is read and acted upon.

Treasurer's Report

The report of the Treasurer is usually called for next, but many small organizations do not require the Treasurer to make a full and detailed report at each meeting. Unless otherwise called for, these clubs require the Treasurer to report only the balance on hand at the last meeting, the receipts and disbursements since the last meeting, and the balance on hand at present. As this report has not been audited, some clubs are satisfied with an oral report from the Treasurer, awaiting a detailed and audited report at the next meeting. This treatment of the Treasurer's report is optional with the club, and need not be made the subject of a By-law. It is merely a matter of customary procedure. Whether a full report from the Treasurer is called for at every meeting, or only at certain specified meetings, it is always well to call for a vote on accepting the Treasurer's report, rather than assuming its acceptance as in the case of the minutes. Unless the Treasurer's report has been audited, it is not necessary to "adopt" it. It is merely read and placed on file.

Reports of Committees

Following the reports of the officers, the Chair will call on the chairmen of the various committees for their reports, usually beginning with the standing committees and taking them in the order in which they are enumerated in the By-laws. (It is wise for the President or the Secretary to check off these committees one by one on the "agenda" which has been prepared in advance for the meeting.)

The President says, "I will ask the Chairman of the Committee on Finance to report." After the report has been read, two courses of action are possible:

If the report does not contain any recommendations for action on the part of the club, nothing further is necessary than to move and vote its acceptance.

But if the report contains recommendation for action (as for example, if the Finance Committee recommends the adoption of a budget for the coming year), something more than mere acceptance is necessary. A member may say, "I move we accept the report of the Finance Committee and place it on file." This means that the report is on record and may be discussed and acted upon later. But the motion may be phrased, "I move we accept the report and adopt the recommendations contained therein," and in that case the membership discusses the advisability of acting as the committee suggests (i.e., adopting the outlined budget), and when the vote is taken, it is taken not on the report alone but on the action recommended in the report. If the report of the Finance Committee is adopted under this kind of motion, the club has adopted the proposed budget and is bound to live up to it.

The same method is used in adopting the report of the Membership Committee. Care should be observed that the distinction is clearly made between accepting the report (placing it on file) and adopting and acting according to the recommendations made in the report, which may mean voting on the admission of new members.

At this meeting there may not be any special committees to report, but where such committees have been appointed and are to be heard from, it is customary to call for them after all the standing committees have been heard from.

If a committee has not had a meeting and has no report to make, it should be called for just the same and the Chairman should reply, "Madam Chairman, the House Committee has no report to make." That committee is then checked off the secretary's list, and thus there is no possibility of any committee being overlooked.

At this point, if an officer or committee has performed some distinguished or outstanding service for the club, it is proper to pass a vote of thanks. Any acknowledgements of this kind are usually placed after all the committees have reported, but the motion to accept the report of a committee, either standing or special, may include a statement of thanks. Thus, if the thanks are included in acceptance of the report, the motion would be stated, "I move that we accept with thanks the report of the Finance Committee"; but if the gratitude of the club is to be expressed a little more significantly, then at the conclusion of reading all the committee reports, a member says, "I move that the club pass a special vote of thanks to the Finance Committee for its successful efforts in raising these much needed funds." Still more significant is to say, "I move that the President be instructed to write a letter of thanks to our Finance Committee for its successful efforts in raising these much needed funds and that a copy of this letter be spread upon the minutes."

If the thanks are carried in the vote, and not written, it is sufficient for the committee chairman or individual receiving the thanks to rise and say, "Thank you," or merely to bow in acknowledgement of the courtesy.

Letters of thanks, condolence, etc., (not included in replies to communications already received as read by the Corresponding Secretary), are in order at this time.

Corrections in Committee Reports

In receiving reports from committees, it sometimes becomes necessary to discuss them in detail, and to make corrections, or ask for further details. If a report calls for correction, a member may rise and say, "Madam President, I move that the Chairman of the Entertainment Committee include in her report an itemized account of the expenses connected with the Patriotic Pageant recently given."

This is discussed pro and con, precisely like any other motion, until the Chair asks, "Are you ready for the question?" Someone in the group answers, "Question!" and the vote is taken. If the motion is carried, the correction is ordered inserted in the report before it is finally filed.

Special Committees

When the club accepts the report of a special committee as final, that committee is automatically dissolved. For example, a committee appointed to take charge of a special program, or a celebration or entertainment is dissolved when the club accepts its final report. For the next special service of this kind, a new committee is appointed. If the club wishes to have all entertainments of whatever kind in charge of one committee, for a year, that can be accomplished by including an Entertainment Committee in the list of Standing Committees as enumerated in the By-laws. Special committees for special functions are better for most organizations.

At times a special committee entrusted with solving some problem or accomplishing some project for the club fails to agree on methods and plans, or fails to complete its work. When asked to report, the chairman of this special committee announces that its members have not completed their task, or that they cannot come to an agreement on a report. A member will then rise and say, "I move that the committee be instructed to proceed further with the work and report at the next meeting," or "I move that the committee be discharged and a new one appointed," or "I move that the committee be discharged and the project dropped."

Unfinished Business

Having disposed of all reports, regular and special, the Chair says, "We will now consider business carried over from the last meeting."

It is quite possible that there is no business carried over from a former meeting, in which case, of course, the presiding officer says that as there is no unfinished business the discussion of the new plans and activities is in order. But there are usually some problems and projects which cannot be finally disposed of in one meeting and so are carried over to the next.

If the unfinished business has been in the form of a motion, duly seconded, upon which no vote was taken at the former meeting, the Chair reminds the club of that fact, and asks the Secretary to read the motion. The question is then open for discussion. It is not necessary for a new motion to be made and seconded, as the first one (at the former meeting) is still valid, not having been voted upon.

Each item of unfinished business must be disposed of separately before the meeting can take up new business.

New Business

After the last item of unfinished business has been taken care of, either by vote, or by decision to defer action till a later meeting, the Chair says, "We are now ready for new business."

The introduction of new business may be arranged for in advance, or it may spring spontaneously out of the meeting itself.

In the former case, the Chair will say, "Mrs. Wallace, will you tell us about the suggestion that the club co-operate with other civic groups in a campaign for the Community Chest this fall."

Mrs. Wallace explains to the club the plans that have already been made, and the Chair says, "Will someone make a motion, in order that we may discuss the proposition?" A member says, "I move that our President appoint a committee of six from this club to co-operate with the Community Chest Citizens' Committee." When the motion has been seconded (and carefully re-stated by the President to avoid any misunderstanding), it is open for discussion and in due time is voted upon.

It may be that the Chair will have upon her agenda for the meeting no items of new business. In that case, she will say, "Is there any new business to come before the meeting?" Any member may then make a motion, but all new business should be put as quickly as possible in motion form. Sometimes in an informal group, a member will say, "I think we ought to do something about all-night parking on the streets," and another member will say, "We ought to have zoning laws for parking, like other towns," and other members will chime in, and an animated conversation will ensue. The tactful presiding officer will know how to cope with this outbreak. She will say, "Mrs. Weber, do you wish to put your ideas in the form of a motion, so that we can discuss them?" Perhaps Mrs. Weber hasn't thought the matter out very clearly and she may not be ready to make a motion, or may not know how to express it clearly. A little friendly counsel and help from her friends and neighbors will be useful, but sooner or later, and preferably sooner, the meeting must be led back to orderly procedure and discuss only those matters which have been brought before it properly, and these matters must be disposed of before other matters are discussed.

When and How to Adjourn

Prompt adjournment at the proper time is very desirable. After the Order of Business has been properly attended to, the

Chairman may say, "Is there any further business to come before the meeting?" If no one claims the floor, the Chairman says, "There being no further business, the meeting stands adjourned," or "A motion to adjourn is in order." If this motion is made and seconded, it is voted upon like any other motion. The motion to adjourn, however, is not necessary, if the Order of Business has been completed and if no one responds to the Chairman's call for any further business.

It is also possible to make a motion earlier in the meeting proposing that the meeting adjourn at a certain specified time. If such a motion is seconded and passed, the time for adjournment is fixed and must be adhered to.

If the meeting is a regular meeting and nothing is said about any special meeting, then it is understood that adjournment means until the time of the next regular meeting and it is not necessary to mention this in the motion. If a special meeting is anticipated, the motion may be worded somewhat like this, "I move that we adjourn to meet one week from today."

Completing the Order of Business and adjourning the meeting does not necessarily mean that all questions have been definitely settled. Many subjects may have been discussed and referred to special and standing committees, which will give further consideration to them and report at later meetings. There may be plenty of unfinished business held over until the next meeting, but this has been done by the judgment of the assembly and not by chance or neglect. Every motion which has been made during the course of the meeting must be disposed of in one way or another before the meeting adjourns. Various ways of holding over unfinished questions will be discussed in a later chapter.

Proper Parliamentary Conduct

In your study and observation of parliamentary law, try to keep in mind a few simple and basic facts. If the proceedings of the meeting seem to become complicated and you feel you have lost the thread of continuity, don't worry. There are details which sometimes are confusing even to experienced club members and occasionally a presiding officer will find that the motions and amendments and other questions before the house have become tangled in a web of words which is difficult to unravel, but this is a rare occurrence. Clubs which have large membership and fear that their meetings may get out of hand, usually appoint a "Parliamentarian," who is an authority on proper procedure. The President may call on the Parliamentarian for advice in a difficult situation, and the advice given by the Parliamentarian must be derived from the book which the By-laws have specified as the authority by which club meetings shall be governed.

Though an expert may be called upon in rare instances, it is not necessary for the average club member, or even club officer, to have a profound and exhaustive knowledge of parliamentary law in order to follow the outlines of a typical meeting.

Remember that no subject is supposed to be discussed until after a motion has been made and seconded. It is then open for discussion, but not until then. If there has been any confusion about the wording of the motion, or any doubt as to its exact meaning, the Chair should ask the person making the motion to repeat it. Sometimes slight changes in wording are suggested by other members, in which case the original maker of the motion should accept or reject the suggested improvements. Equal in importance to the fact that a subject cannot be discussed by a meeting until it has been put before them in the form of a motion properly seconded, is the fact that from that point on *all* discussion must be confined to the question that is under consideration. Any other remarks should be ruled out by the Chair as "Out of order."

(In committee meetings, board meetings, and small groups it quite often happens that a subject will be discussed before it is put in the form of a motion. This is only allowable where the group is small. As soon as it is evident that a common opinion has been worked out, a member of the group makes a motion which is seconded and put to vote. This informal proceeding, however, should never be allowed in a regular club meeting.)

All speakers should rise, otherwise the discussion quickly gets out of control and becomes an animated and frequently confused conversation. In rising to discuss a question, the speaker must address the Chair, and not the meeting. In large groups it sometimes simplifies matters if the member mentions her own name, thus relieving the President of the embarrassment of wishing to recognize a member whose name she cannot recollect. (A quick and reliable memory for names and faces is one of the best assets a presiding officer can cultivate.) If the presiding officer does not know or cannot remember the speaker's name, she may recognize her by saying, "The lady in the second row." Very often the Recording Secretary renders valuable assistance to the executive officer by making a special effort to remember names and faces. She has the roll call of the membership before her and with a little practice can work up a surprisingly full and detailed "card index" in her own memory. This is largely a matter of concentration and practice and as Recording Secretary she does not have as many responsibilities in the conduct of a meeting as the presiding officer and has a little time to practice the fascinating game of "names and faces." Every time any member makes a motion, or a speech, the Secretary mentally checks her name. The list of club membership on the desk before her helps to clarify her mind and jog her memory. Whenever the President hesitates for a name, the Secretary mentions it in a low tone, which need not be heard by anyone in the assembly. Any presiding officer appreciates such help, although of course it should not be forced on any President who does not need it. It is, however, no disgrace for a presiding officer to inquire from the Secretary (*sotto voce,* that is, in a low voice) the name of a speaker, especially in a large group.

It should be remembered that all motions are made by other members than the presiding officer.

Wording of Motions

Another point to be remembered is that the wording of motions should be a matter of care. It is not enough to "get the gist" of the subject of debate and vote. It is necessary to have it exactly right. Sometimes the member who makes the motion does so stumblingly and has to be straightened out. Sometimes the Secretary will have to have the motion repeated. It is a good idea, except for very simple motions, to have the Recording Secretary write out the motion and read it to the meeting, to make sure that it is correctly stated and understood by all. After an extended discussion, the President will ask the Secretary to re-read the motion just before the vote is taken. Failure to state the exact motion and also to state clearly the result of the vote has resulted in confusion in many a meeting. Not only should the motion be read to the assembly just before the vote is taken, but the presiding officer should make sure that the meeting is in order and the members fully aware of what they are voting about.

Methods of Voting

There are several methods of voting, which will be discussed in a later chapter. In most instances, at least at the early meetings of the club which we are now discussing, a *viva voce* (spoken) vote is sufficient, "All those in favor will say 'Aye,' those opposed 'No.'" If this simple formula leaves any doubt as to the preponderance of "Ayes" or "Noes," the next simplest form is to say, "All those in favor signify by raising their hands." The Recording Secretary then counts the raised hands. When this is done, carefully and not hastily, the presiding officer says, "All opposed raise their hands." Again the hands are counted by the Secretary. Still more definite is the method of rising and remaining standing until all are counted. It is essential that both sides of the motion should be called for in the vote—those in favor and those opposed. Sometimes in the excitement of the moment, or in a case of obvious result, the presiding officer will call for the Ayes and forget the Noes. The other absolute essential is that the result of the vote be announced, either, "The ayes have it, the motion is carried," or in more difficult situations the announcement of the actual number voting either for or against the motion.

The Presiding Officer

An efficient presiding officer has responsibilities which cannot always be stated in terms of detailed duties. The spirit of parliamentary law must be administered as well as the letter. The President must know when to be firm (though not necessarily dictatorial) and when to relax the rigors of the law and even perhaps inject a little humor into the proceedings. She must protect the quiet majority from the noisy and contentious minority. She should learn how to bring out the best in a timid speaker and how to check or repress a talkative controversial member. With experience she will learn to think quickly and clearly and express herself succinctly. The result will be poise and a feeling of self-confidence which will communicate itself to her listeners. Above all, the presiding officer must always remember that she stands for a fair and impartial attitude on all questions.

A good presiding officer keeps a meeting moving. Without seeming to impose her will upon an unwilling assembly, she will see to it that there are no awkward intervals and no empty places in the program. If a discussion lags, it can be brought to an end by saying, "Are you ready for the vote?"

Only when she is reasonably sure no further new business is to come before the house (that is, the assembly or meeting), or when she feels that the full time allotted for the meeting has elapsed, should the Chair call for adjournment.

III

Constitution and By-Laws

CERTAIN items must be included in any Constitution and By-laws, therefore the following discussion will cover all the essential points. When a club is being organized, one of the most important things for the organizing group to do is to appoint a committee to draw up a Constitution and By-laws, and this committee must consider each of the items in turn and make such decisions in regard to them as will best serve the interests of the new club. The general form and purpose of the club must be clear in their minds when they set to work, and the Constitution and By-laws which they draw up must fit the particular needs of their club, and should not be merely an imitation of the Constitution and By-laws of some other club.

Provision is made for the alteration of both Constitution and By-laws, so that you may benefit from experience and make such changes and modifications as may be necessary to adapt this outline to the needs of your own organization.

The Purpose of Constitution and By-Laws

The Constitution lays down the fundamental principles on which the club is to operate. The By-laws establish the rules of guidance by which it is to function. The By-laws may be more easily amended and altered than the Constitution, because methods of procedure should be made capable of adaptation to changing conditions.

Outline of Constitution

ARTICLE I—NAME

This club shall be called The ——————— Club of ———————

ARTICLE II—PURPOSE

The purpose of this club shall be to bring together at frequent intervals those who are interested in civic betterment of any nature, with the purpose of promoting the cause of good citizenship. For this purpose we shall study history, sociology, civics, public health, community recreation and other topics which may improve local conditions and create more friendly and sympathetic relations in club and community, and we shall also take such practical action as may seem wise and desirable to us after such study.

It is advisable to state the purposes of the club as to general principles, but not to go into too great detail or to limit it too definitely. As time goes on and the club grows in experience as well as in membership, its purpose may be somewhat altered from the original plan without losing its main character. Many organizations have become more and more extensive in their activities and have gone on sometimes for several years in enthusiastic and successful pursuit of ideas and projects which were later discovered to be outside the range of purpose outlined in the Constitution and hence (in a sense) illegal. This required an amending of the Constitution and in some cases an amendment of the charter granted by the State, a long and complicated process. If your proposed club is of a kind (such as a Good Citizenship Club) which will take active part in public affairs, and thus come in contact with town, county, and state authorities (such as school boards, library boards, domestic relations courts and other legal aspects of community life) it might be well at the start to have your Constitution and By-laws read over by a lawyer.

ARTICLE III—MEMBERSHIP

The membership shall consist of not more than fifty women, and shall be open to any women of the community interested in the purpose of the club.

Here are some debatable points for your Committee to decide before submitting the proposed Constitution to the club. Should the membership be limited in size or should it be allowed to expand as far as its natural tendencies take it? As a matter of general principle it may be said that if the activities of the club will touch on all phases of community welfare the membership should be unlimited. If under these circumstances it outgrows its original modest home or auditorium, larger quarters can be obtained when the time comes. If the membership is to be unlimited, you may provide in the Constitution for two classes of membership: *Active members* have full participation in all the deliberations and activities of the club; *Associate members* pay smaller dues than active members and may attend meetings and listen to discussions, but have no vote in the organization and cannot hold office. If your club plans to do work for civic betterment or for improving social conditions, associate members may be called Contributing members.

If the purpose of your club is not as broad as outlined above, but is more specialized, or is strictly cultural and social in character, membership should be limited. Thus a League for Civic Betterment might be unlimited in membership, while a Thursday Morning Music Club might be limited.

ARTICLE IV—OFFICERS

Section 1—The officers of this club shall be a President, a Vice-President, a Recording Secretary, a Corresponding Secretary, a Treasurer, and an Auditor.

Do not try to limit your official group to two or three individuals. It is better to have too many officers, than too few. Concentration of power in a few hands always arouses suspicion and antagonism. Even though some of your officers are not as efficient as they might be, it is better to be patient and to try to train them in their duties rather than to let one person, no matter how willing and efficient, do all the work. One secretary might be able to keep the minutes and attend to all the correspondence, but in the long run you will find it better to divide the two aspects of secretarial responsibility. Most people like to hold office and have a title of some kind, and you may sometimes subdue antagonism and win a friend by appointing a possible malcontent to office or at least to Chairmanship of a committee.

The office of Auditor is unnecessary if provision is made for an audit of accounts by a paid professional accountant not less than once a year. Such an audit is not a reflection on the honesty and efficiency of your Treasurer. An honest and efficient Treasurer will probably demand an annual audit.

Section 2—The officers shall be elected by ballot at the May meeting each year to serve for one year. They may be re-elected for one additional term.

It is usually wise to provide for a limitation to the terms of office of the various officers, thus preventing the control of the club from falling into the hands of a small clique. One year is perhaps too brief a tenure of office,—sometimes it takes almost a year to train a good executive or secretary,—but in some cases one year proves to be the best term of office.

ARTICLE V—EXECUTIVE BOARD

Section 1—There shall be elected annually from the active membership of the club three members who shall meet with the officers of the club to formulate plans and decide all purposes and procedure of the club. These three members, together with the officers of the club, shall constitute the Executive Board. They shall be elected at the annual meeting, shall serve a term of one year, and shall not be eligible for re-election for more than two consecutive terms.

With five officers (if you decide to do without an auditor) and three other members of the Executive Board, you have a small group which will act as a steering committee for the whole club. The advantages of having such a group are that they will be able to meet more often, to deliberate more concisely, and to act more decisively than the larger and more varied body of the club membership. The Executive Board will function chiefly during the intervals between the meetings of the club itself. At such times it may sometimes act for the club, but it should always be remembered that the Board is subordinate to the club and must carry out its instructions, and cannot take any action conflicting with any action taken by the club or with its avowed purposes. In case of conflict, the club can countermand any action taken by the Board, and can give it instructions. One of the most useful things an Executive Board can do is to reduce problems of procedure to their simplest elements and present the situation to the club for ultimate decision. The Executive Board is sometimes called the Board of Directors or the Executive Committee.

Section 2—Vacancies occurring among the members of the Board shall be filled by election by the Executive Board, such officers or Board members to serve only until the next annual meeting.

An exception may be made if a vacancy occurs during the club year in the office of President, in which case the Vice-President may succeed to the office. If this is not specifically stated in the Constitution, the office of President must be filled by election by the Executive Board as outlined above, unless there is a provision requiring that vacancies be filled by vote of the members as a whole.

ARTICLE VI—MEETINGS

Section 1—The club shall meet regularly on the first and third Wednesday afternoons of each month from September to June, inclusive, at places designated by the House Committee.

Nothing could vary more widely than the times and places of club meetings. You may meet once a week, once a month or once a year, but your Constitution should make some provision for regularity, so that the club can carry on its corporate life under fairly fixed conditions and not at the mercy of varying circumstances or the whim of any individual.

Section 2—The regular May meeting shall be the Annual Meeting for hearing reports from all the officers and standing Committees and for electing the same.

The purpose of holding the Annual Meeting in the spring is to give the newly-elected officers an opportunity during the summer to formulate their plans and have everything in readiness for the first meeting in the fall. Officers and Standing Committees may take office at the June meeting, or this may be made the occasion of a résumé of the preceding year's work by the outgoing officers.

Section 3—Special meetings for special purposes may be called by the Executive Board at such times as are thought advisable. Such special meetings may transact only such business as is specified in the call, and special meetings may not supersede regular meetings except when especially provided for.

ARTICLE VII—AMENDMENT

Any proposed amendment to this Constitution may be submitted in writing at any regular meeting of the club. Such proposed amendment must be signed by three active members of the organization before being submitted to the meeting, and shall be read to the meeting by the Recording Secretary. After such notice, it may be voted on at the next Annual Meeting and shall become a part of the

Constitution only if approved by a two-thirds majority of the members present and voting at said Annual Meeting.

One of the purposes of having a Constitution is to provide a form of procedure which may not too easily be changed. Any amendment to the Constitution should be carefully considered and a certain amount of time should be allowed between the date of its proposal and the date of its adoption. The Annual Meeting is the best time for the final decision, as this meeting will probably be attended by the members who are most likely to give careful and constructive thought to the development and best interests of the club.

Outline of By-Laws

The Constitution lays down the basic principles of the organization; the By-laws concern chiefly methods of procedure rather than basic principles. By-laws are more easily amended than the Constitution and their amendment need not in any way affect the main purpose of the club.

The following suggested By-laws are intended to include all the necessary rules for club action, but your own particular set of circumstances may require other By-laws not included in this general scheme.

In this chapter we are discussing only methods of procedure in connection with officers, membership, etc. In a later chapter we will consider the personal qualifications which you should look for, not only in the selection of your officers but in your membership as well.

I—Membership

Section 1—Names of proposed new members shall be submitted to the Membership Committee in writing. Each name shall be proposed by one member and endorsed by two other members who know the candidate personally.

Section 2—All names of candidates for membership who have been passed unanimously by the Membership Committee shall be recommended to the club at a regular meeting. A favorable majority vote of all those present and voting at such meeting shall be acceptance of the candidate for membership in the club.

Some organizations permit the Executive Board to accept or reject candidates for membership, but in most instances it is better to have the names presented to the full membership of the club as represented at a regular meeting.

Some organizations which wish to preserve their private and exclusive character have a rule that one adverse vote is sufficient to disqualify a candidate for membership. If such a rule is adopted, it is necessary that the voting be done by secret ballot. Unless there is some definite reason for such drastic rule, however, candidates for membership should be accepted by a *viva voce* vote at a regular meeting. It may safely be assumed that candidates passed by the Membership Committee and recommended to the club are suitable for membership.

Section 3—If at any time a member wishes to resign from the club, she shall give notice of such intention in writing to the Membership Committee (or to the Executive Board)—(*Choose one method*.) After having been approved by the Membership Committee (or the Executive Board) the resignation shall be presented to the club and acted upon in the same manner as prescribed for joining the club.

II—DUES

Section 1—The initiation fee shall be ———.
The annual dues shall be ———.

There is ample opportunity for disagreement here, and the Committee on Constitution and By-laws should consider carefully all the various factors involved before submitting this By-law to the club. You may not wish to have any initiation fee at all, although this is customary in nearly all organizations.

Or you may wish to admit the original or charter members (those attending the organization meeting) without payment of initiation fee, but collect such a fee from those joining later.

The amount of the annual dues is something on which no outsider can advise you.

Section 2—Annual dues are payable on or before ———.

This date should be selected in order to give your club the maximum use of the funds in its treasury. As most organizations are more active in fall and winter than in summer, it is probably advisable to make October 1st or November 1st the deadline for payment of dues. In planning a budget for a year's work, and in making a financial report on past activities, it is customary to follow the outline of club activities rather than the calendar year. As far as your Treasurer is concerned, January 1st is just like any other day, but the day on which she has to bring her year's tenure of office to an end and make a report of receipts and expenditures is an important one. This adaptation of the calendar year to organization needs is called the "fiscal year." If your club is inactive during the summer months, it will probably be advisable to set the beginning of your fiscal year as May 1st, or June 1st, with dues for the ensuing year payable on or before October 1st or November 1st.

Section 3—Members who have been declared in arrears in the payment of dues shall not be eligible to vote.

This could be expressed another way, "Only members whose dues have been paid are eligible to vote," but this might be awkward or embarrassing to some members who carelessly allowed their dues to become a few days or weeks in arrears. A more diplomatic procedure would be to add to the above By-law a second sentence, as follows: "Members who have failed to pay their dues within thirty days (or sixty days) of the date on which such dues became payable shall be declared to be in arrears." This gives the Treasurer an opportunity to send a second bill, or at least to make a tactful suggestion to the careless member.

Section 4—Any member whose dues have not been paid for six months from the date on which they were due may be dropped from membership by a majority vote at any regular meeting.

This is an important rule. Its force may be strengthened by saying "shall be dropped" instead of "may be dropped."

No member whose dues are in arrears may be allowed to resign from the club. If the amount of dues in arrears is not paid, the member should be dropped for non-payment of dues.

On the other hand, the resignation of any member whose dues are not in arrears *must* be accepted. The member may be asked to reconsider the resignation, but if she declines to withdraw the resignation, the club has no alternative but to accept the resignation. The reason for this rule is apparent when you consider that the club has no right to insist upon a member continuing to pay dues after having resigned, and also that if the dues become in arrears through no fault of the member (who has sent in a resignation and is therefore no longer liable for dues), it is manifestly unfair to drop the member later on because the dues have not been paid.

Section 5—Any member who has been dropped from membership because of non-payment of dues, or who has been absent from club meetings for one year or more without adequate excuse shall not be reinstated until she has been re-elected and has paid dues in full from the date at which they became delinquent.

This rule may seem overly severe in some cases, but it is almost universally followed in all organizations. If you wish, a somewhat different arrangement may be made by providing a By-law which reads, "shall not be reinstated until she has been re-elected and has paid the regular initiation fee exactly like a new member."

Section 6—No cancellation or refund of dues shall be made if a member resigns before the close of the fiscal year.

III—Duties of Officers

These By-laws prescribe the specific duties of officers. Further remarks on their personal qualifications for office and advice as to the conduct of affairs will be found in Chapter IV.

Section 1—President. The President shall preside at all meetings at which she is present; shall exercise general supervision over the affairs and activities of the club; and shall serve as member ex-officio on all standing committees.

If the President desires to participate in debate, she may turn over the chair to the Vice-President or such other officer as she shall select.

Section 2—The Vice-President shall assume the duties of the President during her absence.

In some clubs it is considered advisable for the Vice-President to be a member ex-officio of all standing committees, just as the President is. Other clubs have the Vice-President an ex-officio member of some committees but not of others. This should be specified in the By-laws according to your own judgment.

Section 3—The Recording Secretary shall keep the minutes of all meetings of the club which shall be an accurate and official record of all business transacted. The Recording Secretary shall also be the custodian of all club records unless a special officer shall be appointed for that purpose.

Some clubs require the Recording Secretary to be an ex-officio member of all standing committees, together with the President and Vice-President, but this seems unnecessary in most organizations. The records which the Recording Secretary keeps are those of the club as a whole, not the records of committees, either standing or special. The Committee records enter the record of the club only after they have been passed upon by the whole club.

For the keeping of important documents, mementos, and other important properties concerning the life of the club, some organizations have an officer called Historian, Archivist, Librarian or some similar title. If you wish to have such an officer, provision should be made in the By-laws, with responsibilities and limitations of the office clearly defined.

Section 4—The Corresponding Secretary shall conduct all correspondence of the club.

This refers, of course, only to correspondence of the club as a whole and does not include correspondence (more or less official) of the various officers and chairmen of committees.

Section 5—The Treasurer shall receive all club funds, keep them in a bank or repository selected or approved by the club and pay out funds only on an order signed by the President and Secretary (or Chairman of the Finance Committee.)

Some organizations do not consider it necessary to specify the bank or banks in which club funds are to be deposited, but in the long run this is a formality which may save misunderstanding and embarrassment.

It is highly important that all disbursements from the club funds be made only on written order or "voucher" signed by at least two officers.

Section 6—The Auditor shall examine the records of the Treasurer and certify their correctness to the club not less than once a year.

Some organizations elect two Auditors; others do not elect official Auditors from their own membership, but employ a paid auditor from outside club membership. No matter by what method the correctness of the accounts is certified, it is important that this should be done at least once every year. Sometimes a semi-annual audit is preferred.

IV—Executive Board

Section 1—The Executive Board of the club shall consist of the officers of the club and three Directors elected by the club as provided by Article V, Section 1 of the Constitution. The duties of the Executive Board of the club shall be ———.

The powers of the Executive Board should be clearly indicated. In some organizations the Executive Board has power to conduct all business of the club. This often causes criticism from members of the club who feel that the Executive Board is carrying on dictatorially and that they themselves have nothing to say about how the club shall be run. A safe provision is to state that the Executive Board shall consider, promote, and transact the business of the club subject to instructions of the club at a business meeting or subject to approval of the membership as expressed by vote at a regular business meeting. In any case, it is wise to have a By-law stating clearly just what the Executive Board can and cannot do.

V—Committees

Section 1—Committees shall be appointed by the President. All Standing Committees, after appointment by the President, shall be ratified by the club at a regular business meeting.

Election of committees is usually a cumbersome and not very satisfactory process. It is better to have them appointed by the President, but in order to avoid any suspicion of dictatorial methods, important committees (such as Standing Committees which hold office during an entire year) should be ratified by the entire membership of the club as expressed by vote at a regular meeting.

Each club should create such Standing Committees as seem to be necessary for its work. Special committees can always be appointed at any time, as need may arise.

Any committee either appointed or elected should have its powers clearly defined.

Section 2—The Standing Committees shall be as follows:
Finance
Membership
Program
House
Nominating
Resolutions
Hospitality

The first three are essential; the others may be omitted at the beginning and added later if thought advisable. Even if you have no club-house, a House Committee is still an important and valuable aid to the organization. Such a committee has the responsibility of selecting suitable meeting places and preparing them for club meetings.

The Nominating Committee may be a special and not a standing committee. However, even though it may function only once a year, it may be classified as "standing."

Resolutions are always important functions in any club. A Resolutions Committee can render important service by collecting, editing, and re-wording proposed resolutions before they are presented to the club for action. All resolutions should be submitted to the Resolutions Committee and no resolution should be presented to the club until it has first passed through the hands of the Resolutions Committee. One important reason for this is that it prevents needless repetition. The Resolutions Committee, however, should not have power to act for the club in passing resolutions. Its functions are purely editorial and advisory.

VI—QUORUM

Section 1—Fifty-one per cent of the membership shall constitute a quorum for the transaction of business.

The question of quorum is extremely important. It is necessary to have all transactions of the club approved of by a sufficient number of members to avoid disputes and disagreements, otherwise a small group of club members could meet, pass resolutions, vote money, and take other action in the name of the club without the consent and concurrence of the full membership. In the case of a small club a majority of the membership (fifty-one per cent or more than one-half) may constitute a quorum necessary for transaction of business. In larger and more diversified clubs a smaller proportion may be agreed upon. Some organizations require only one-fourth of the total membership, but if a fairly representative group of members may be expected at regular meetings, it is much wiser to provide a larger quorum. If a small group gathers at the beginning of the meeting, even though a full quorum is expected later no official action can be taken until the quorum is actually present, although the smaller group can conduct informal and unofficial discussion. If an important matter is to come up at any regular meeting, it is desirable to make sure in advance, as far as this is possible, that a quorum will be present.

VII—ORDER OF BUSINESS

Section 1—The order of business at all meetings of this association shall be as follows:
1. Meeting called to order
2. Roll-call
3. Reading of minutes of previous meeting
4. Reports of officers and committee chairmen
5. Unfinished business
6. New business

7. Program (addresses and entertainment)
8. Adjournment

The roll-call is necessary to establish the fact that a quorum is present. The minutes of the previous meeting should be approved by vote if correct or should be corrected if found to be inaccurate in any way. The reports of officers and committee chairmen should also be approved and inserted in the records by vote of the club. All unfinished business should be attended to before new business is taken up, even if "attended to" means only that the unfinished business cannot be definitely disposed of and must be continued to later meetings as "unfinished." It should never be ignored, but must be mentioned before new matters are brought up. An act of adjournment should be taken,—the meeting should not be allowed to break up informally. If no other date is specified, the act of adjournment means until the date of the next regular meeting.

In many clubs adjournment takes place before the program of the day. If a social hour follows instead of a serious program, adjournment should always precede it. A formal adjournment is sometimes difficult to achieve (if not actually impossible) after a social hour, or a program of purely entertainment value. The type and character of your club will help you to decide whether you wish to adjourn the business meeting and then have the entertainment, or whether you wish to listen to a serious address or debate and then (perhaps after a discussion of the program and the passing of resolutions or appointing of committees in response to whatever appeal has been made), take formal adjournment. In the latter case, the program is part of the regular meeting and must be reported in the minutes as having taken place, although it is not necessary that the program be reported in detail.

Some clubs and social organizations like to have a ritual or litany, which is usually performed immediately after the roll-call. This ritual may consist of the singing of a hymn (such as "America the Beautiful"), or the recitation by all present of the "Salute to the Flag," or some other idealistic and inspiring "text" in conformity with the purpose of the club.

VIII—Parliamentary Authority

Section 1—Robert's *Rules of Order, Revised* shall be the parliamentary authority for this club.

There must be one, and only one, authority for all questions of parliamentary procedure, not only in order to find out in advance how to act under any given circumstances, but also in order to settle any disagreements or misunderstandings as to past actions. The rules codified years ago by General Henry M. Robert have been a standard authority for many organizations.

IX—Amendment

Section 1—Any amendment to these By-laws may be proposed at any regular meeting, to be adopted by a majority vote at the following meeting, if, in the meantime, the proposed amendment receives the approval of the Executive Committee.

It will be observed that the By-laws may be amended (and this includes adding to and subtracting from their number) somewhat more easily than the Constitution.

Method of Adoption of Constitution

In reporting to the organizing group of a new club, it is customary for the Chairman of the Committee on Constitution and By-laws to read the entire proposed Constitution, and at its conclusion to say, "Madam Chairman, I move the adoption of the Constitution as just read." After this motion has been seconded the Temporary Chairman says, "It has been moved and seconded that the Constitution be adopted as read. The motion is now open for discussion."

The Chairman of the Committee which has drafted the Constitution and By-laws then retires to her seat in the assembly, leaving the manuscript on the desk. The Secretary then rises and re-reads the draft of the Constitution, article by article. Each article of the Constitution is then discussed in order. Changes may be recommended and, if approved, inserted in the report, but the Constitution is not finally voted on until each and every article has been discussed. It should not be necessary to vote on whether or not an article should be changed. The sense of the meeting and its approval or disapproval of any article can easily be obtained by the trend of the remarks made.

When the proposed Constitution has been thoroughly discussed, the Chairman says, "Are you ready for the question?" Silence will give consent or one or two members may say, "Question." The Chairman then puts the vote and announces the result. By this vote, the Constitution is accepted or rejected as a whole.

If there is serious difference of opinion on the Constitution, the Committee may be given further time to revise it and to bring it nearer to the desires of the club. In that case, of course, the vote to adopt the Constitution as read will result in the negative; and the Committee will be expected to take sufficient time to make the required revisions, reporting later at the same meeting, or at a meeting set for a later date, whichever the circumstances require. If the Constitution, as read and discussed, is acceptable, it is adopted by *viva voce* vote, which is usually made unanimous. Whatever disagreements may have arisen during the discussion are now smoothed out and forgotten. The dissenting minority bow to the will of the majority and there should be no "Noes" in the final vote.

The Constitution having been accepted, all those who desire to join the proposed club sign the Constitution, pay their initial dues (or agree to do so), and become *founders* or *charter members* of the organization.

Method of Adoption of By-Laws

The Chairman then calls on the Committee on Constitution and By-laws to make its report on the proposed By-laws. The same procedure is followed for the By-laws as for the Constitution. The By-laws are presented by the Chairman of the committee, re-read one by one by the Secretary, and discussed one by one by the assembly. The vote for acceptance or rejection, however, is on the By-laws as a whole and not individually.

IV

Duties and Qualifications of Officers

SELECTION of officers requires careful consideration of the various duties and responsibilities involved. Some people are unsuited by temperament and habit to assume responsibility,—they are enthusiastic followers, but not leaders. Others make a fine start but a poor finish,—they are incapable of sustained effort. A good President may make a poor Secretary, and vice versa.

The small club has not so great a range of choice as the larger one, but on the other hand the small club is more apt to be united in purpose for any one line of study and action, and the members will probably have much in common. A larger club, with service to the community as its aim, will probably represent many ways of thinking and many different types of people. This enlarges the range of possibilities for responsible office-holding, and while it may increase the problems, it also increases the opportunities.

A growing club should select its new members with care. Membership should be considered from the viewpoint of mutual benefit to the members and to the club itself.

Individuals who are invited to join the club should be made fully aware of the purpose of the organization, and should accept a place in it because of their willingness to co-operate with that purpose. Qualities of loyalty and helpfulness as well as willingness to co-operate and to assume individual responsibility are taken for granted and will undoubtedly develop as time goes on. Out of new members, as well as from charter members will emerge individuals who will assume leadership in various ways.

In selecting officers, it is advisable to sound out the proposed nominee as to her ability or willingness to serve. Never place a name in nomination before the club until it has been ascertained if the member is willing to serve if elected.

Personal charm and popularity should not be ignored in making your selections, but these attributes should never be the prime considerations. Social obligation should never be paid off by nomination for club office. The main consideration should always be ability and willingness to serve the club. Personal vanity or ambition to shine may induce an individual to seek office, and these characteristics can be put to good use, but you should be reasonably sure that the ambitious candidate for office has other and more dependable qualities. At the opposite extreme you will find many modest and self-effacing individuals who will at first shrink from the idea of attracting any of the limelight to themselves, but often these relatively obscure members of the club will have the very qualities of industry, pertinacity, and dependability for which you are looking,— qualities which will develop amazingly if you are willing to follow your own judgement of the character of these members and entrust responsibilities to them. Some knowledge of the daily lives of your members is necessary, especially for this first official board. For a women's club, a capable, well-balanced woman who manages her home well, or a teacher or business woman who shows the qualities necessary to hold a job and advance in the world,—these are likely candidates for official responsibility.

President

Let us consider first the qualifications which go to the making of a good President. To a large degree, the President will typify to the outside world the club itself. She is its representative as well as its leader.

Some people are born leaders, others attain leadership by long and patient effort. But the quality of leadership must be there, either actual or potential, in your choice for President.

Leadership is not necessarily the ability to turn out prodigious quantities of work, but rather the ability to inspire others to work with and for you. Leadership cannot be bought with wealth or social position. It may include a striking personality, a good platform presence, eloquence, and personal charm, but it lies in something beyond and above these qualities. Leadership is sometimes dependent upon an almost indefinable quality, something subtle and intangible. It is a quality which engenders faith and inspires confidence. If your founding group does not contain any individual in whom these qualities are outstanding, keep them nevertheless in mind and see if they do not develop with experience and authority.

A prime requisite for a President is to be a good presiding officer. This means that she must have the ability to think clearly and fair-mindedly, to be firm as well as impartial. The President must have sufficient knowledge of parliamentary law, and a close familiarity with the Constitution and By-laws of the particular club. But the ability to preside is not all that is required. You should not sacrifice a good leader in order to get a good parliamentarian. An appreciation of the larger purposes and an ability to stick to a definite course over a period of time will do more for the club than an ability to handle meticulously the petty details of organization life.

The President should know enough parliamentary law to conduct business legally and promptly, with fairness to all, but she should also have the ability to see the club as a whole and not as a partisan of any group and she should have a clear vision of its ultimate purposes and possibilities.

As a presiding officer, the President should set an example to the assembly in fairness, courtesy, and obedience to rules. The atmosphere of the club meetings is largely a reflection of the personality of the presiding officer.

The definite duties devolving upon the presiding officer are to call the meeting to order promptly at the appointed time; to announce the business before the assembly in its proper order; to state clearly and to put properly all questions brought before the meeting; to announce the result of each vote and the next business in order; to inform members on points of order, and to answer parliamentary inquiries relating to pending business when necessary to enable members to proceed in order; to preserve order and control debates; to receive all messages and to announce them to the assembly; to name the members (when directed to do so in a particular case, or when it is made part of the President's duty by a rule) who are to serve on committees.

The presiding officer personifies and represents the group, declaring its will and in all things obeying implicitly its commands. While exercising leadership of the assembly, the presiding officer is also its obedient servant.

For answering questions of legality and proper procedure, the wise presiding officer will have a copy of the Constitution and By-laws on hand for prompt consultation and decision. The authoritative book on parliamentary law (By-law VIII, Section 1) should also be available, although any lengthy pause in the proceedings to look up a fine point should be avoided if possible.

The presiding officer should maintain strict impartiality. She takes no part in the debate and has no vote in the assembly. If for any reason she wishes to take part in a debate, she must call someone else to the chair. This may be the Vice-President or any other officer or member of the assembly. This temporary presiding officer is called the Chairman or President *pro tem* (that is, *for the time*). The presiding officer, however, should be very cautious about leaving the chair and joining in any debate. By doing so (especially in cases where strong feeling has already been manifested), she destroys the confidence of the opposite side in her impartiality. Under no circumstances should she resume the chair until the question at issue has been disposed of, as it would be highly improper for her to put to vote a question on which she herself has taken definite sides.

If the tally of votes on any question results in a tie, the presiding officer may vote. (See page 102.)

A gracious Chairman who tries to keep everybody happy and greets all problems with the same smiling acquiescence may not have the force of character necessary to be a good presiding officer, but on the other hand a grim-faced Chairman whose chief interest is in enforcing strict adherence to the letter of the law (sometimes at the expense of its spirit), may not be a good presiding officer either. The ideal lies somewhere between these two extremes.

Some presiding officers do too much of the talking themselves. It is the function of the presiding officer to conduct and guide debate and not to dominate it. Impartial and voteless, she lets others do the talking, but has and should exercise authority to stop aimless discussion and she should insist at all times that speakers stick to the point.

This is not always as easy as it might appear. What can be done with the overly-talkative member and the chronic objector? Tact and firmness must be combined. The obstructionist must be silenced with the least possible amount of hurt feelings. Sometimes the first step is for the presiding officer to rise (she usually remains seated during debates), and at the first opportunity remind the long-winded member that everyone must have a fair chance in the debate and no one should exceed a fair and courteous time-limit. If this does not bring about the desired result, the presiding officer may address the assembly somewhat as follows: "Is it the sense of the meeting that this matter deserves fuller discussion or do you wish to bring the debate to a close?" This will frequently bring a motion that the discussion be closed. Or the presiding officer may suggest that as the time allotted for discussion of this particular question has ended and it is necessary to go on to further business, a motion to lay this question on the table, or to defer it to a later meeting, is in order.

Ability to keep her head through all vicissitudes and upheavals is an important quality in a presiding officer. Sudden and unexpected crises may arise, often from petty causes. Sometimes a capable presiding officer will see trouble in the offing, and will head it off tactfully. Sometimes she must choose between two members both of whom want to talk at once. Whichever one is first recognized as having the floor, she must invariably see that the second member has an opportunity immediately after.

Another important function is to see to it that the affairs of the assembly are conducted without dragging. A prompt beginning is necessary, but is only half the battle. Business must be kept moving, or boredom and loss of interest are the inevitable result.

Second in importance to a prompt beginning is a prompt ending. All public speakers, lecturers, musicians, actors,— "guests of honor" of various kinds,—sooner or later come up against the long-winded dilatory club which cannot bring its business meeting to an end in time for the distinguished guest. If you interview a group of distinguished speakers who have had much experience with clubs, you will undoubtedly find that this is their chief criticism and cause of complaint. Sometimes it is necessary for them to curtail their talk in order to catch a train, and sometimes they are so bored and exasperated at the long wait that they cannot bring themselves into the proper frame of mind to do justice to themselves or to you. When the distinguished guest is waiting at the back of the hall, or in a drafty ante-room and the appointed time for his or her appearance has come and gone, the capable presiding officer should be absolutely ruthless in terminating debate and bringing the meeting to an end.

The President who meets successfully the responsibilities which devolve upon her as presiding officer will have plenty of opportunity to exercise those gifts of mind and personality which have guided her in her public appearances in private and more personal contacts. For one thing, her executive abilities will be put to a test early in her term of office in making committee appointments. Wisely chosen committee chairmen will go far toward making a successful club year. Proper committee appointments require thought as to the work which the committee is to do and selection of the person best suited to that particular work.

During the months following the new President's election (these are ordinarily the summer months when the club is not meeting) she should give careful study to the needs and purposes of the organization and should endeavor to work out a practical plan for the coming season. She may confer with the officers and directors, either collectively or individually, and should insure co-operation from them in any plans she may develop.

Above all, the President should have dignity. She cannot

afford to listen to gossip or to take part in political or personal quarrels. She is President of the entire club, not of any one group or faction.

Vice-President

Nominating Committees sometimes underestimate the importance of the Vice-Presidency, regarding the office as purely honorary and selecting for it someone unsuited for important responsibilities. It is true that some Vice-Presidents are merely figureheads, but this is not a proper use of the office.

The most important thing to remember in selecting a Vice-President is that she may be called upon to take the place of the President at any time and so should possess many of the qualities which have guided you in the selection of a President. In practically all organizations, the Vice-President succeeds automatically to the Presidency if at any time the President is not able to finish the full term of office. Illness, death, or resignation from any one of many possible causes may remove the President from activity, and the Vice-President must be prepared to carry on. No By-law is necessary for this succession in office.

Some societies have several Vice-Presidents each of whom has charge of a special department of work. In case of the death or resignation of the President, the Vice-President becomes President, the Second Vice-President becomes First, the Third becomes Second, and so on, unless the By-laws provide differently.

A really capable Vice-President takes the office seriously. She may be a figurehead or a valuable assistant leader, as she herself chooses. If she aspires to succeed the President—in many clubs the Vice-Presidency is considered the training-ground for the next President—she will endeavor to cultivate in her own personality the qualities which distinguish the President; she will study the policies of the administration and help to carry them out; she will familiarize herself with the basic principles of parliamentary law and also the Constitution and By-laws of the club so that she will be able to preside wisely and firmly in the absence of the President.

In order to prevent any possibility of the Vice-President being merely an unnecessary and useless accessory to the organization, it is wise to assign her certain definite tasks, especially the Chairmanship of an important committee. Appropriate standing committees for a Vice-President to head are Finance, Program, or Resolutions, because these committees are concerned very definitely with policies of administration. An energetic and capable Vice-President may be chairman of more than one committee, although in most cases it is advisable not to group too many committees under one head.

Recording Secretary

Next to the President, the Secretary is the most important official in the organization. The relationship between the President and the Secretary is a very close one and it is important that these offices should be held by individuals who can work together harmoniously and with common purpose. The President must depend upon the Secretary not only for official co-operation but also for a multitude of inconspicuous and more or less personal bits of information, advice, and sympathetic aid. In most clubs the Secretary is not only the President's "right bower," but also a kind of "general utility" officer.

As the duties of the Recording Secretary are very definite and permit very little leeway for personal idiosyncrasies, the qualifications which go toward the making of a successful Recording Secretary are easily recognizable. As she is custodian of the permanent records of the society, she must be accurate and painstaking. As she keeps the minutes of meetings, she must be a person who is habitually prompt. (Detailed discussion of how to prepare and keep proper minutes will be found in Chapter VI.)

As she has to read minutes, she should have a good clear voice and be able to make herself heard and understood.

At each and every meeting she should be able to produce quickly the minutes of preceding meetings, the list of members and their addresses (to keep such a list correct and up-to-date is no small task in itself), and also a copy of the Constitution and By-laws. For the convenience of the Chair, the Recording Secretary will have the order of business, including a list of the committees which are to report at the meeting, together with the names of the chairmen. To keep these papers in order on her desk and to have them readily available is an important attribute of a capable Recording Secretary. It has been said that a true sign of the qualifications of the Recording Secretary is the way she handles the papers on her desk. Nothing is more distracting than a pause while the Secretary scratches hastily through her papers for a document which should have been produced at once when called for.

The records of the Secretary should always be up-to-date and in order, so that they will be open to inspection by any club member.

It is the duty of the Secretary to read to the assembly all papers, communications to the club, etc., when called upon to do so.

The Secretary has need for a clear voice and a good manner of speaking, not only for the reading of the minutes, but also for calling the roll, and for counting votes when voting is done by raising hands or by rising.

Corresponding Secretary

In small clubs, the duties of the two secretaries may, if desired, be combined into one office.

Where there is a secretary for correspondence, she should cultivate facility in writing and courtesy of phrasing, also neatness in writing or typing letters. In this mechanical age, every club secretary should have a typewriter and be able to use it expertly.

All letters should be written on stationery bearing the club's name, address, and list of officers. The address of the Corresponding Secretary should always be prominent in the letterhead.

The Corresponding Secretary should keep all correspondence received, properly filed under appropriate headings, and should keep with each letter received a copy of the reply.

The Corresponding Secretary notifies chairmen and members of committees of their appointment and defines the purpose of the committee as set forth in the By-laws or by action of the club. She sends out notices of meetings and writes letters of congratulation or condolence on motion of the assembly.

The Corresponding Secretary acts only for the club as a whole. Officers and Chairmen of committees conduct whatever correspondence may be connected with their respective duties. Invitations to all guests of honor are written by the President, and she answers personally any similar invitations which she may receive. All letters concerning unpaid dues or collections and disbursements of money are the duty of the club Treasurer.

The Corresponding Secretary must have a considerable amount of discretion as to what is proper and what is not. However, she should never use club stationery for personal correspondence, and she must always be careful not to make statements or express personal opinions in a letter written on the club letterhead which might in any way involve the club in controversy or reflect on its dignity.

Treasurer

The office of Treasurer requires very special qualifications, and the club Treasurer should be selected with the greatest care.

It goes without saying that your Treasurer should be honest and dependable. Some societies require that the Treasurer be bonded, but in most cases this is unnecessary. The Treasurer will act for the society only upon due authorization. Every transaction must be accompanied by a document of some kind. Bills for dues should be properly receipted. All expenditures should be accompanied by a voucher signed by at least two properly constituted officials. Cancelled checks may be considered as proper receipts for club money disbursed, although a signed receipt in addition to the cancelled check is advisable.

If possible, choose a Treasurer who has had some business experience and is familiar with handling money and accounts. Club accounts may not be very complicated and can be easily mastered by anyone with a clear and logical mind, but a little experience along this line will be a big help. Like the Recording Secretary, the Treasurer will be called upon to make reports (usually at every regular meeting) and she should be able to stand up in public and speak distinctly and intelligibly.

The preparation of a budget for a year's expenditures is a task belonging properly to the Finance Committee. The Treasurer will work with the Finance Committee and will abide by its rulings.

Promptness in acting upon the club's instructions is an important asset for a good Treasurer and will do much to establish the club's position in the community. Bills should be paid promptly and accounts kept carefully so that the monthly balance report from the bank can be easily and quickly checked.

A more detailed description of the Treasurer's duties will be found in Chapter IX.

Executive Board

The Executive Board or Board of Directors acts as a connecting link between the officers and the general membership of the club. Membership on the Board carries definite responsibility, and directors should be made to feel that they are important in the structure of the organization.

In electing directors, clubs may well use the opportunity to try out promising but less experienced members who will thus become familiar with the policies and business procedures of the club. Membership on the Board should be regarded as a kind of training school from which club officers of the future will be chosen.

Your directors, elected from the general membership, should represent all groups in the club, should be in sympathy with the aims of the club, and as anxious to promote its growth and welfare as the officers themselves.

V

How Motions Are Made and Amended

SOME KNOWLEDGE of the principles underlying the use of motions is necessary, not only for officers, but for the members of any corporate body, in fact it may be said that the subject of motions is the most important phase of parliamentary law.

All club business is conducted by means of motions.

The house cannot take any action, transact any business, appropriate money for any purpose, or discuss and vote on any question which has not been presented as a motion.

This chapter outlines all that either officers or club members ordinarily need to know about motions. A more technical analysis of the subject will be found in the Appendix, in the Summary of Parliamentary Law.

To the new club member, motions and amendments form the most puzzling feature of parliamentary procedure; but do not be dismayed if your study of the subject seems to involve you in unfamiliar technical details. Remember that experience is a far more valuable teacher than theory. A sure technique in the use of motions is not to be gained entirely by studying books. It is in the actual use of motions that their form and purpose become clear. It has already been suggested that it is good to try out the use of parliamentary law in an informal group-practice. Each person present in turn takes the part of presiding officer. Any motions can be made and seconded,

amended, and discussed. For instance, "I move that we appropriate $50 toward co-operating with the Kiwanis Club in build-
ing a public swimming pool at Lincoln Park." "I think we
ought to find out what the Kiwanis Club has already done in
this direction. I move that the President be instructed to appoint
a committee to confer with the Kiwanis Club and report back
to us at the next meeting."

Is this correct? If not, why not? Each question as it arises
can be first discussed by the group. An hour or two spent in this
fashion by a small group of congenial spirits will be highly
instructive.

Making a Motion

A motion is a proposal that the assembly take action, or that
it express itself as holding certain opinions.

A motion may be made by any member of the assembly
(except the presiding officer). The member first obtains
recognition from the presiding officer by standing and waiting
until acknowledged by the Chair.

The presiding officer "recognizes" a member by announcing
her name, or in small assemblies, where all are known to each
other, by merely nodding the head in her direction. If two or
more members rise at approximately the same time, the Chair
must decide which rose first, or use her own discretion as to
which is to be recognized first.

Presumably the member has formulated the correct wording
of the proposal which she wishes to bring to the attention of
the meeting. She says (after being recognized, or "obtaining
the floor"), "I move that" or "I move to."

Do not say, "I make a motion that,—"

For the sake of absolute accuracy, a motion may be put in
writing, read by the one who proposes it, and handed to the
Recording Secretary. (Some large assemblies insist on having all

main motions, the adoption of which would commit the assembly to any definite viewpoint or action, made in writing, but for smaller and more intimate groups, this is not necessary.)

It is very important that the exact wording of the motion be understood by all. To make this clear, the presiding officer frequently repeats the motion, inquiring from the proposer if the wording is correct.

Seconding a Motion

A motion *must* be seconded in order to be considered. In other words, the proposal must interest at least two members of the assembly. If a motion is not seconded, no notice whatever need be taken of it by the presiding officer, but for the sake of absolute fairness to all (a cardinal principle of good presiding), the Chair may say, "It has been moved that—so-and-so. Is the motion seconded?" If no seconding is forthcoming, the Chair says, "The motion cannot be considered," and proceeds with business as before.

Seconding a motion is expressing approval and interest (at least for purposes of discussion) by one other member than the proposer. It is customary for the proposer to rise, but it is not necessary for the seconder to rise, although in a large group it may be advisable.

Two or more seconds may be made to any motion, although one is enough.

When a motion has been made and seconded, it is then stated to the assembly by the presiding officer and thus becomes a subject for discussion and decision.

Until a motion has been stated to the house by the Chair, it cannot properly be discussed or acted upon, nor can any other motion or speech be made by any member following the recognition by the Chair of the member who first rose and made the motion.

When moved, seconded, and stated from the Chair, a motion cannot be withdrawn or ignored, except where the original mover asks for permission from the assembly. No other member can ask to have a motion withdrawn (although it can be disposed of in other ways, as will be described later), and to be strictly formal and legal, a motion after it has been stated by the Chair can be withdrawn *only* by a motion made and seconded and voted on as in other cases.

When a motion is regularly before an assembly and is being discussed, it is the duty of the presiding officer to re-read or re-state the motion as often as asked to do so by any member.

Types of Motions

Motions are of two kinds, Main and Secondary. An understanding of this simple but sometimes confusing distinction is essential for good parliamentary procedure.

Main Motions

A main motion is one which introduces a subject to the assembly.

A main motion is debatable and is also amendable,—that is to say, the opinions of those present may be expressed in regard to it, not only by their votes, but also by their words. Expression of opinion by members in orderly debate serves the purpose of not only clarifying the issues, but also of influencing undecided members. It is quite proper for any member in favor of a motion to present all the arguments he or she can think of which seem to make the action advisable and to present those arguments as persuasively as possible. The opponents have the same privilege. Only the presiding officer must remain absolutely impartial.

To say that a main motion is amendable is to say that it may be changed by some addition or modification.

DIAGRAM OF PARLIAMENTARY MOTIONS

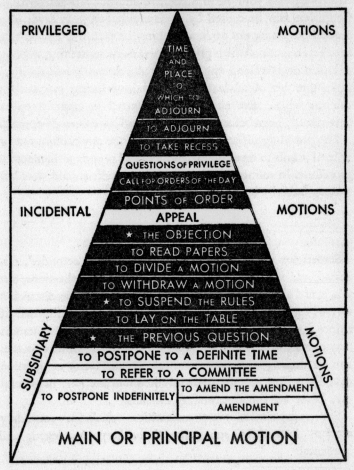

PRIVILEGED   MOTIONS

TIME
AND
PLACE
O
WHICH TO
ADJOURN

TO ADJOURN

TO TAKE RECESS

QUESTIONS OF PRIVILEGE

CALL FOR ORDERS OF THE DAY

INCIDENTAL   MOTIONS

POINTS OF ORDER

APPEAL

★ THE OBJECTION

TO READ PAPERS

TO DIVIDE A MOTION

TO WITHDRAW A MOTION

★ TO SUSPEND THE RULES

TO LAY ON THE TABLE

★ THE PREVIOUS QUESTION

SUBSIDIARY   MOTIONS

TO POSTPONE TO A DEFINITE TIME

TO REFER TO A COMMITTEE

TO POSTPONE INDEFINITELY   TO AMEND THE AMENDMENT

AMENDMENT

MAIN OR PRINCIPAL MOTION

THE WHITE SPACES DEBATABLE MOTIONS   *MOTIONS REQUIRING TWO-THIRDS VOTE.
THE BLACK SPACES UNDEBATABLE MOTIONS

A bit of advice to the proposer of a motion may be in order. Always express yourself in a positive and not a negative form. Confusion may be caused by an assembly voting in favor of a motion proposing *not* to do something, or even worse by voting to defeat a motion which proposed *not* to do something, making a double negative and implying that the assembly *will* do it.

Another bit of advice is to avoid introducing motions on subjects which have already been referred to committees, or have already been before the assembly and have been postponed.

The presiding officer has the right to rule any motion out of order if it fails to meet the requirements of proper parliamentary procedure. In ruling a motion out of order, she should state her reasons tactfully but definitely.

Secondary Motions

Sometimes a main motion will be proposed, seconded, discussed, and voted upon without any further complications, but this is not always the case. During the course of the discussion various questions may arise which will have to be disposed of before the main motion is voted upon, or other circumstances may occur which make a vote on the main motion inadvisable; and for dealing with these situations certain forms of question have from time to time been invented and are now in general use. These are called secondary motions.

For convenience, most authorities sub-divide secondary motions into three sub-groups: subsidiary, privileged, and incidental.

Subsidiary Motions

Subsidiary motions are those which are made while another motion is pending, for the purpose of properly disposing of that other motion. The subsidiary motion supersedes the other motion for the time being, and must be acted upon before action can be taken on the other motion.

(1) For instance, some members may consider the proposal one which should not be acted upon at that particular time and someone may move that the question be postponed indefinitely. That is a subsidiary motion and, if seconded and voted upon favorably, puts an end to the main motion without the latter having been brought to a vote. In other words, the club has evaded a decision for the time being, but this does not necessarily mean that the original proposal has been voted against. It can be revived at a later meeting by being proposed again as a new main motion.

(2) The general principle of the motion may be approved, but the form in which it is presented may be considered unsatisfactory, in which case a motion to amend may be made. This also is a subsidiary motion and must be considered and voted upon before the main motion is decided. (See page 72.)

(3) It may be felt that more information is needed and that the proposition should be studied more carefully than can be done in an open meeting. A motion is then made to refer the question to a committee, which is instructed to report at a later meeting.

(4) Perhaps the hour is growing late, or it may be felt that the proposal is too important to be decided hastily and that there should be more time for thought and discussion on the part of the members, and yet it is not the desire of the meeting to postpone decision indefinitely. The usual motion in that case is to postpone to the next meeting, or some other meeting. (This is not to be confused with postponing indefinitely.)

(5) If the discussion threatens to become long-winded and tiresome and if the issue is sufficiently important that many members show an inclination to express their opinions, a subsidiary motion may be made to limit the time of debate. This

motion should be made to fit the needs of the situation. For instance, "I move that members be allowed to speak only once on this question, not to exceed two minutes." The time limit for debate can thus be shortened, but it can also be lengthened if occasion seems to warrant. Perhaps one member shows an unexpected or unusual knowledge of the problem involved and the members want to hear more than a two-minute speech. In that case a subsidiary motion is made, "I move that Mrs. Gordon's time be extended to ten minutes."

(6) A subsidiary motion which is sometimes made and which is apt to be confusing to those not familiar with parliamentary procedure is: "I move the previous question." The object of this motion is to stop debate and to prevent the introduction of any further amendments. This "previous question" motion cannot be debated or amended. The presiding officer puts it to vote (provided it has been seconded). Parliamentary practice requires a two-thirds vote for the adoption of this subsidiary motion, so the vote should be counted carefully, either by raising hands or by rising. If the assembly votes in the affirmative, the debate is ended, and vote taken on the main motion. If the assembly rejects the "previous question" motion, the debate goes on.

(7) Another way of postponing decision on a main motion is the motion to "lay it on the table." This is different in purpose than the motions to postpone to a certain date or to postpone indefinitely. To lay on the table usually means a more or less temporary deferment, with the privilege of resuming consideration at any time when no other question is pending, if a majority wish to do so. On account of its temporary nature, the motion to lay on the table takes precedence over all other subsidiary motions. It cannot be debated or amended. When seconded, it must be put to vote at once.

It will be seen that all these possible circumstances conform to the definition of the subsidiary motion. They grow out of the main motion and are put to vote before the main motion which they affect. It should always be kept in mind that the subsidiary motion does not in itself take the place of the main motion. For instance, a motion to postpone or to lay on the table, if defeated, leaves the main motion just as before. A motion to amend also, if defeated, leaves the main motion just as it was originally presented.

Privileged Motions

Privileged motions, like subsidiary motions, are entitled to take the place of any other motion or proposition which may be under consideration, and must be acted upon and decided by the assembly before the pending motion,—but unlike subsidiary motions, they do not grow out of the main motion. Privileged motions have (in themselves) nothing to do with the pending question, but they are of such importance that they are allowed to interrupt the consideration of other questions, hence the well-deserved title, "privileged."

Privileged motions are not debatable.

(1) The most privileged of all privileged motions is the motion to adjourn. It takes precedence over all other questions whatsoever.

It is sometimes said that a motion to adjourn is always in order, but this is not quite true. If a motion to adjourn has just been made and defeated, it is obviously out of order to make another, otherwise members wishing to interrupt the debate and hinder the transaction of business could keep on making motions to adjourn almost indefinitely. Other times when a motion to adjourn is not in order are when a member has the floor and is speaking, or when the time for adjournment has already been established, or when the assembly is considering the time and place of the next meeting, or when a vote is in process of being taken.

If the motion is simply to adjourn, it is not debatable and is not subject to any subsidiary motions. But if the motion is to adjourn until a certain definite time and place, it may be debated. If no date is specified, the adjournment (if taken) is until the next regular date.

(2) The questions next in relative importance superseding all others for the time being, except that of adjournment, are those which concern the rights and privileges of the assembly itself or of the individual members. For instance a member may rise and at an opportune moment say, "Madam Chairman, we who are sitting in the back row cannot hear the report now being made. Will you kindly ask the speaker to speak a little louder?" Or sometimes, during a long discussion, a member may interrupt for a moment to ask if a window may not be opened, or closed. It is sometimes necessary to ask for quiet during a discussion. Whatever the cause, the individual members have a right to rise and say (without waiting for recognition from the Chair), "Madam Chairman, I rise to a question of privilege." The Chair considers whether the question is of sufficient importance to be complied with, and acts accordingly, and the interrupted business is then resumed.

Questions of privilege are of course not strictly speaking "motions," but they are interruptions of such a character as to justify their inclusion among the privileged motions. The Chair may grant the privilege, or put it to a vote if an objection is made.

(3) Another privileged motion is technically known as "the orders of the day." Business should always be taken up in order, and if for any reason the meeting strays away from the proper procedure, a member may rise and say, "Madam Chairman, I call for the orders of the day."

Note that the word is "orders" and not "order." This means the whole procedure for the meeting, and not any one subject. (A "point of order," however, is a *point* concerning the *rules* governing the meeting.)

The call for the orders of the day is highly privileged. It needs no second, cannot be debated or amended. It should not be made, of course, unless the assembly has very obviously upset the proper procedure, or unless the presiding officer has been negligent. It may possibly be that the assembly prefers to continue the discussion in which it is engaged. After the call for the orders of the day has been made, the presiding officer says, "The orders of the day have been called for. As many as are in favor of proceeding to the orders of the day say Aye. Those opposed No." If the question is decided in the negative, the assembly continues whatever work it is engaged in, and the call for the orders of the day cannot be made again until the subject under consideration has been disposed of.

Incidental Motions

Incidental motions are of various kinds, arising out of other questions, and should be disposed of before continuing with the subject in hand.

(1) For instance, questions of order (that is, "points of order"); of appeal from any decision by the Chair; of temporary suspension of the rules in order to consider any specific question out of its usual order or for any other apparently valid reason; these are all incidental motions.

(2) Objection to the consideration of any main motion by any member may be made, provided the objection is made before the debate has begun. The member rises and says, "Madam Chairman, I object to the consideration of this question." The Chairman immediately says, "The consideration of this question

has been objected to. Does the assembly wish to consider it? All in favor of the consideration say Aye,—opposed No." Unless the Noes prevail by two-thirds, the objection is voted down and the consideration goes on.

(3) If a vote is taken *viva voce* and there is any doubt in the mind of any member as to the result, he may call for a counting of the votes. This call must be made immediately after the vote has been taken before another subject is introduced, but once made it has precedence and the count must be made. The best means of accomplishing this is to have those voting in the affirmative rise and remain standing until counted by the presiding officer or recording secretary or both, then after they are seated, the opposing voters rise and are counted in similar manner.

(4) Requests of various kinds rising out of the business of the meeting are considered as incidental motions and are to be disposed of before proceeding with the business in hand. For instance a member may rise and say, "Madam Chairman, I rise for information," or "I should like to ask the speaker a question."

The presiding officer is not supposed to answer all questions from members in regard to parliamentary law, but occasionally a member has a question to ask which is really important or necessary in order to know how to vote. "Madam Chairman, does voting in the affirmative on this question commit the club to definite action or does it merely express our opinion," or "Are we voting now on the motion as originally made, or as amended?" These, and others like them are fair questions, and should be answered at once.

It will readily be seen that incidental motions are well named. They are incidental to the main business of the assembly and may arise and be disposed of at almost any stage of the proceedings. They have no definite rank (such as we have described for main, subsidiary, and privileged motions). They are in order whenever they are incidental to the business in hand and they must be decided before returning to the pending question or before any other business is taken up.

Incidental motions are not debatable (except an appeal from a decision by the Chair), and most incidental motions are of such a nature that they cannot be amended.

Amendments

In the discussion which follows the introduction of a main motion, suggestions may be made as to changes in the wording of the motion. These changes are called amendments. Where the changes involve only minor alterations in the wording of the original motion, it is sometimes the practice for the mover of the proposition to which the amendment relates to signify consent to the proposed change and for the amendment to be made without any question or vote being taken by the assembly.

More often, however, the suggested alteration involves a more important change than mere wording. In that case a motion to amend is made, seconded, discussed, and voted upon as a subsidiary motion. If accepted (i.e. voted upon favorably), the original motion is thereupon considered as changed and when voted upon is decided in its amended and not its original form. If the amendment is defeated, the main motion stands as it was originally proposed, just as if no amendment had been offered.

Suggested amendments may be friendly to the original motion, or antagonistic to it, and must be carefully considered and discussed before being brought to vote, otherwise the whole purpose of the main motion may be defeated by a carelessly worded amendment.

The presiding officer should always make it clear to the assembly that it is the amendment which is being discussed and voted upon, and not the main motion.

All amendments to a main motion (so far as form is concerned) may be effected in one of three ways:

(1) By inserting or adding certain words;

(2) By striking out certain words;

(3) By striking out certain words and adding or inserting others.

For instance, a motion may be made, seconded, and stated by the presiding officer, that "a committee of three be appointed to confer with the Kiwanis Club in regard to the proposed swimming pool and report at the next meeting."

AMENDMENT #1, I move that the motion be amended by striking out the words, "and report at the next meeting." (Seconded) The discussion is then whether or not the committee should be required to report at the next meeting. After the discussion, the vote is on this question of the committee's report, not on the appointment of the committee. Let us suppose that the amendment is voted upon *favorably*. In that case the committee (if appointed) need not report at the next meeting.

AMENDMENT #2, I move that the motion be amended by adding the words, "by the Chair," after the word "appointed." (Seconded) The discussion and vote then concern whether the committee should be appointed by the chair or by some other method not specified.

AMENDMENT #3, I move that the motion be amended by striking out the word "three" and inserting the word "five."

Each one of these motions is discussed and voted upon separately. If there are no further amendments proposed, and no further discussion of the main motion, it is put to vote as originally proposed (if all the amendments have been voted down) or in its altered form (according to which amendments were acted upon favorably).

An amendment to a main motion (such as those just mentioned) is called a primary amendment. While one primary amendment is being considered, no other primary amendment to the main motion may be considered.

However, after one primary amendment has been voted upon, another primary amendment may be offered. There is no limit set by parliamentary law as to the number of primary amendments which may be proposed, provided, of course, that they are not repetitious and that they all relate to the original main motion.

During the discussion of any primary amendment, a suggestion may be made as to an alteration in the amendment itself. This is called a secondary amendment (or an amendment to an amendment). It must be moved, seconded, discussed and voted upon, just like a primary amendment, but when disposed of, the primary amendment is the subject before the house, and not the original main motion. After one secondary amendment is disposed of, another secondary amendment may be proposed, but no amendments to secondary amendments are possible, as it would be manifestly absurd to go on amending amendments indefinitely.

Control of Debate

While primary and secondary amendments are being discussed and acted upon, it is very important for the presiding officer to keep strict control of the debate. Where several amendments are offered on a debatable question, members of an assembly are apt to become confused and will sometimes vote on an amendment under the impression that they are voting on the original main motion, and sometimes this results in a decision exactly opposite to what they intended. Even at the risk of seeming repetitious, the presiding officer should always state very clearly just what is under discussion, and should insist firmly on only one phase of the subject being discussed and voted upon at a time, returning at last to the main motion.

"Out of Order"

Another duty of the Chair is to rule "out of order" certain amendments which may be proposed. The Chair should be careful to exercise this authority with discretion, as most amendments which will be proposed are in order, but occasionally one will be offered which (probably quite unintentionally) upsets the whole orderly processes of group action. For instance, an amendment may have nothing whatever to do with the original motion; or it may turn a positive motion into a negative one by some such simple process as moving to insert the little word, "not"; or it may go back over ground already covered by striking out or inserting words which have already been considered and acted upon.

No motion is in order which conflicts with the avowed object or purpose of the organization.

No motion is in order where the group has no jurisdiction; for instance, "I move that we have mail delivery on Sundays and holidays."

VI

How Resolutions Are Made

RESOLUTIONS are akin to main motions, in that they propose that the club officially express an opinion or take action, but they are different in form from motions and are handled differently. Resolutions are so important that they are entitled to a chapter by themselves.

Motions can be made by any member of the assembly. Resolutions can be presented to the assembly only after being passed by the Resolutions Committee, which should be a Standing Committee.

Types of Resolutions

A resolution ordinarily corresponds to one of two types. One type expresses the club's policy or point of view on a question of public interest. A resolution of this sort, passed by a club, may carry much influence among the public and legislators.

The second type of resolution is a pledge on the part of the club to perform a certain piece of work.

Every resolution, even those expressing merely the opinion of the club, and not specifically committing it to group action, should carry with it at least the implied pledge of the group and the individual members to help in carrying the expressed opinion of the organization into effect.

Form of Resolutions

Resolutions always follow a certain form, consisting of two parts. The first part sets forth the conditions underlying the situation with which the resolution is concerned; the second part should grow logically out of the first part, and expresses the opinion of the club. The first part is always introduced by the word "whereas," and the second part, "therefore be it resolved." Both parts should be expressed as forcefully and succinctly as is compatible with a full statement. More than one "whereas" is allowable and most resolutions contain more than one such statement. "Be it resolved" may also be used more than once, but above all things repetitiousness must be avoided and all unessential matter eliminated. This is especially true of the first part. Too many "whereases" cut down the force of the resolution, and too frequent use of "be it resolved," thins out the effect of the resolution. Have a clear presentation of the target to be aimed at, use as few shots as possible, and your chances of hitting the bull's eye are greatly increased.

Let us suppose that a member submits the following resolution to the committee:

"Whereas the elementary schools in the Second Ward are crowded to a point endangering the health and safety of the pupils; and

"Whereas, the pupils in three grades are now receiving only part-time instruction; therefore be it

"Resolved, that the Century Club place itself on record as demanding that the city authorities immediately rent additional rooms and take action toward building new school houses in the Second Ward, and be it further

"Resolved that a copy of this resolution be sent to the Mayor, the Board of Education, and the press."

The resolution, signed by the member or members who drew it up, is submitted to the chairman of the Resolutions Committee, who brings it up at the next meeting of the committee. If the matter seems particularly urgent, the chairman may call a special meeting of the committee.

The resolution as prepared meets the requirements which we have already mentioned. It concerns a matter of public interest, and is presumably within the avowed scope and purpose of the club. The Resolutions Committee will satisfy itself that the facts are substantially as stated and that the schools in question are really overcrowded and that certain groups of children are really receiving only part-time instruction. The two underlying conditions which are criticized are presented briefly, with no unessential matter, i.e., the overcrowding is inimical to health and safety and the instruction for which the public pays is not satisfactory. The two courses of action are also clearly stated,— that a demand be made upon the proper authorities for action and that the action of the club be made a matter of public news.

The subject matter may involve another committee of the club, such as Child Welfare, or Public Health, or Education. If any such committees exist, the Resolutions Committee consults them as to their knowledge of the conditions set forth in the resolution and any plans which they may be considering for dealing with it.

Duties of the Resolutions Committee

The importance of having a standing committee which considers all suggested resolutions is something that has been proved by experience. It is a subject which requires careful thought and a certain continuity throughout the year. A special committee appointed for a brief period can hardly be expected to bring the knowledge and experience which are necessary for a proper consideration of resolutions, but a standing committee which meets more or less regularly and which considers all the suggested resolutions is in a position to formulate and follow a consistent policy and to consider new resolutions in the light of past experience.

The task of the Resolutions Committee is not to provide an ample supply of resolutions for the club meetings. On the contrary, a good Resolutions Committee sifts out the suggested resolutions, rejecting all those which seem inadvisable or irrelevant, and presenting to the assembly only those which are of sufficient importance to justify discussion and action.

On no other subject is inexperience quite so apt to go astray as on resolutions. It is so easy to give vent to a sudden outburst of enthusiasm or disapproval by means of a resolution, and it is so easy to get an affirmative vote on it by the assembly, that a word of warning must be our approach to the whole subject. Cynical club members sometimes call the Resolutions Committee the "Hot Air Committee." Clubs, independently and collectively pass resolutions enthusiastically approving of this and that, and heartily disapproving of something else, and all too often the action has no real significance. The club is frequently expressing itself and taking sides in public issues on which it is very poorly informed and with which it has no firsthand contact. It is just a matter of a few "whereases" and a "be it resolved," and an "Aye" vote as a momentary emotion sweeps the crowd, and that is apparently the end of it.

But unfortunately that is not the end of it. Every resolution should be a pledge on the part of the club to carry the opinion of the organization into effect, and many resolutions contain an explicit pledge to do so. Your group should never be allowed to feel that they have done something worth while by merely passing a resolution. A definite statement of opinion on a question of public interest by an influential club may carry much weight in the community. Politicians and other interested parties are not slow to take advantage of this fact, and unless you are careful you may find that your organization has been made use of in a way which may be humiliating or distasteful to you later on. To guard against being imposed upon, a Resolutions Committee which has the experience as well as the knowledge to handle such situations is invaluable to your club.

In order to guard against the injudicious and indiscriminate use of resolutions, some clubs limit the number of resolutions which may be passed to a certain number for the year. Perhaps this is too drastic a remedy and it might very possibly hinder rather than help. A wise and discriminating Resolutions Committee can be trusted to pick and choose among the resolutions brought to its attention and present to the club for approval or disapproval only those which are well-founded on reliable knowledge of the situation involved and concerning something relevant to the purpose of the club and worthy of its consideration.

No resolution should be considered by the Resolutions Committee which has been presented by any individual or group not included in the membership of the club. The subject matter may be suggested by outsiders as worthy of the club's consideration, but no matter how worthy the cause, the resolution must be sponsored by a member.

Submitting Resolutions to the Club

The Resolutions Committee decides that the matter is of sufficient importance for the consideration of the club and reports the resolution at the next meeting of the club.

When the Resolutions Committee submits a resolution to the club for consideration, it does not necessarily mean that the committee itself is in favor of the opinion or action which the resolution represents. It only means that the committee has decided that the resolution is of sufficient importance to warrant the club's attention.

If the proposed resolution concerns a subject on which the club already has a committee, the Resolutions Committee should consult with the members of the other committee before bringing the resolution before the assembly. For instance if you have a Committee on Child Welfare and someone proposes a resolution urging a town ordinance prohibiting children under twelve years of age to attend motion picture houses unaccompanied by adults, the Resolutions Committee will confer with the Child Welfare Committee as to the advisability of such a resolution and the best manner of handling it. In some cases the resolution is brought before the assembly by the special committee (in this case Child Welfare) with the approval of the Resolutions Committee. But the Child Welfare Committee has no right to present such a resolution to the assembly as a result of its own deliberations, without first securing the consent of the Resolutions Committee.

Resolutions must be presented to the assembly in written form. The best method is to have them typewritten and there should be at least two copies, one for the Recording Secretary and one for the Chairman of Resolutions. The typed resolution may be signed by the individual or group proposing it, but this is optional. A third copy of the typewritten resolution may be posted on a bulletin board, or extra copies may be made and passed around among the members of the club so that they will have a chance to study the resolution and think about its various implications before voting on it.

After the resolution has been read to the club and a copy handed to the Recording Secretary, a motion is made and seconded that the resolution be adopted. The question is then open for discussion. Amendments may be proposed, discussed, and voted upon in the usual way.

Safeguarding Resolutions

Some clubs require more than a majority vote to pass any resolution dealing with legislation, local, State, or Federal, placing the minimum of required votes at two-thirds, or even in some cases three-fourths. This By-law, like the one limiting the number of resolutions per year, is not only to safeguard the organization itself, but also to impress members with the seriousness of endorsing legislation or placing themselves on record in favor of measures whose sponsors may have a personal interest in the pending bills.

Any member of the club may propose a resolution, just as any member may make a motion during the progress of a meeting. The restriction placed on resolutions is that they must first be considered by the committee and may not be presented directly to the club. The member proposing the resolution may formulate it in the usual form, or may merely suggest the underlying idea to the committee and allow the committee to formulate the exact wording. In that case, of course, the resolution, when properly worded, should meet with the approval of the original proposer. The committee has also the right to suggest changes in the wording of the resolution, which must be approved by the proposer before being brought before the assembly.

To further safeguard the use of resolutions, some clubs include in their By-laws a provision that no important resolution involving the club in questions relating to public affairs can be voted upon at its first presentation, but it must be read at one meeting and discussed and voted upon at the next. This again may prove to be a drastic remedy for the evil of ill-considered resolutions. A competent Resolutions Committee may be depended upon to give sufficient study to any proposed resolution so that the club learns to have confidence in its judgment. Not only will the Resolutions Committee submit only proposed resolutions which are worthy of the club's consideration, but it will also in the course of its study assemble a sufficient array of facts and figures to hasten the discussion when the question comes before the assembly. Then, it is also possible to defer final decision on an important resolution until the next meeting, whenever the discussion shows a division of opinion, a lack of information, or any other need of more intensive study before the club commits itself on the question.

Importance of Resolutions

If the resolution, either as originally presented or as amended by the assembly, is passed, it becomes a part of the official record of the club. Copies are typewritten, signed by the President, Recording Secretary, and Chairman of the Resolutions Committee, and sent to the authorities mentioned in the resolution.

If the Resolutions Committee decides that the proposed resolution should not for any reason be submitted to the club and if those who originally suggested it are still convinced that it is a matter upon which the club should put itself on record, they may bring up the question at a regular meeting of the club and a motion may be made that a resolution concerning overcrowding in the public schools be considered by the club. As this is over-riding the decision of the Resolutions Committee (and this should be made clear to the club), it requires a two-thirds vote of the assembly to secure its consideration.

If passed by the club, the resolution carries with it the implication that the individual members will do what they can to help solve the problem of overcrowding.

Publicity for Resolutions

An important element in this kind of resolution is the resulting publicity. Both the club itself and the proper solution of the problem of overcrowding will benefit by the right kind of publicity. A club which keeps itself well-informed on public affairs, which puts itself on record in well-thought-out resolutions, and which follows up its expression of opinion by action, will soon come to have a strong influence in the community. On the other hand, a club which passes all kinds of resolutions with good intentions but poor judgment, will receive less and less attention in the newspapers and will soon carry no weight whatever in the community.

Final copies of the resolution as passed should be sent not only to the newspapers, but also to city officials and to others whose support is desired. These copies should be typewritten, using one side of the paper only. They should bear the names of the officials of the club who signed the official copies of the resolution. In copies used for publicity these signatures need not be handwritten but may be typed.

VII

How Minutes Are Kept

THE MINUTES are the official record of the actions of the club at regular or special meetings. As they are official, they cannot be changed after they have been approved by the club. It is of the utmost importance that they be complete (as to essentials), accurate, and clear. Any ambiguity in the wording of the minutes may be a cause of trouble later on. The minutes may be referred to at any time to settle disputes, to provide information, or for any other adequate reason, and they may be offered as evidence in a court of law if necessary.

The minutes of the organization are written by the Secretary, and are in charge of the Secretary. It has been suggested (see Chapter II) that whenever possible the club should have two Secretaries, a Recording Secretary and a Corresponding Secretary. It is the Recording Secretary who is custodian of the minutes, and it is the work of that officer which will be discussed in this chapter. (The duties of the Corresponding Secretary will be discussed in Chapter XII.)

In the absence of the Recording Secretary, the minutes may be kept by the Corresponding Secretary or someone appointed temporarily by the President.

Necessary Materials

The best type of book in which to keep the minutes is a fairly large loose-leaf book. The Recording Secretary keeps careful notes during the progress of the meeting, from which the actual minutes are written after the meeting. These minutes are not written in the book, but are kept on separate sheets of paper until the next meeting. If there are any corrections to be made, they can be made on the separate pages, and when this has been done and the minutes approved by the club they are then transcribed (preferably typewritten) on the proper pages and inserted in the minute book. In this way the minute book is free from any marks of correction, whether of additions, subtractions, or changes of words. This is more than a mere matter of neatness. Any corrections in the minutes after they have been inscribed in the book immediately raise a doubt as to their accuracy.

Another check on accuracy is to have the pages to be inserted in the minute book numbered by a numbering machine. This is accepted as evidence that nothing has been added to the minutes after they have been approved, and nothing taken out.

The minutes as approved and entered in the official book should be written on one side of the page only, appearing in the book on the right side.

The use of the loose-leaf book permits the inclusion of certain papers that are not included in the official minutes, such as a detailed report, a letter from an important personage, or even an important paper read before the club. These can be inserted in the book by punching holes in the proper places, or by transcribing.

Minutes should be written in short paragraphs, preferably with headings, or marginal divisions. When they are written in this form they show at a glance just what they carry, and any special point may be located with a minimum of time and effort. The short paragraphs help toward the same end.

At the end of the year, the minutes of all the meetings may be removed from the book and bound together as a permanent record. In this way, it is not necessary for the Recording Secretary to keep an enormous tome of records, most of which have become ancient history, while more are being added. Also the binding in yearly periods makes future reference much easier.

What to Include and What to Omit

Minutes are a record of all business transacted, including plans presented, activities undertaken, and findings reported at meetings. The minutes should emphasize "all things done and passed," and should minimize what is merely said. Some organizations follow the tradition that their minutes contain only actual deeds or actions, making no mention of things merely proposed or moved without coming to a vote, and leaving out practically all personal references. This is probably sufficient for the bare record, but makes cold reading. But for most clubs, where the social element is never entirely lost sight of, it is advisable to include names of the proposers of important main motions, with occasionally some reference to the principal features of the ensuing debate. The Secretary must develop her own style, and follow her own judgment as to the most suitable form of minutes for the particular organization.

Literary style, however, should be discouraged in a Secretary, except in so far as literary style consists of saying briefly and clearly just what happened and nothing more. A good Recording Secretary is a good reporter, but not a "sob sister," or a writer of special articles for the Sunday papers.

Even where the minutes are a little more than a bare skeleton outline of deeds done, the Secretary should be careful not to allow them to express her own opinions, whether complimentary or otherwise. Qualifying adjectives and adverbs and comments on papers or addresses do not belong in the minutes. Do not say, "Mrs. Jamison read an excellent and carefully prepared paper on 'Library Extension Work,' which was both fascinating and instructive." It is to be taken for granted that the papers are all "excellent" and "carefully prepared" and that they are fascinating and instructive, and if they by any chance do not deserve these compliments, the Recording Secretary would not say so in the club minutes, of all places.

The Recording Secretary should not hesitate to ask questions during the course of the meeting if there is any doubt in her own mind as to the exact wording of a motion or an amendment, or the name of a proposer of a main motion, or any other detail which should become a part of the minutes. The need for accuracy far outweighs any slight interruption of this kind. The names and duties of all newly appointed committees should be set down correctly at the time and not left for future verification.

In clubs where the minutes contain some reference to the discussions and not merely the outcome of the voting, it is permissible for the Secretary to ask to be allowed to read her impression of the sense of the meeting before adjournment, so that she may incorporate it in the minutes before too much time has elapsed to guarantee accuracy.

All rulings of the Chair that may be of value as a precedent should be entered in the minutes. Answers to parliamentary inquiries should also be recorded. Future reference to these decisions and answers may make it unnecessary to consider the same problems again.

Minutes of Committee Meetings

Committees (standing and special) do not as a rule keep minutes of their meetings, although where very important matters are under discussion they may do so if they wish, appointing some member of their own group to act as secretary. If such committee minutes are kept, they are not included in the minutes of the club itself and are not the responsibility of the Recording Secretary. But although committee minutes are not included in club minutes, committee reports *are* included, and it is very important that all such reports be written out and handed to the Recording Secretary exactly as read before the meeting and accepted by it.

Such committee reports, if properly prepared (typewritten on a page not greatly different from the pages of the minute book), may be inserted in the minute book just as handed to the Secretary at the meeting. This original copy, signed by the chairman of the committee, is incontestable evidence of the accuracy of the minutes in that particular. Sometimes a painstaking Secretary who cares greatly for uniformity and neatness in her records will retype the committee reports in the final approved minutes, but in that case it is just as well to keep the original reports on file for a reasonable length of time, just in case some question may arise in regard to them.

For the Permanent Record

After the minutes of any meeting have been approved and inserted in the minute book, they should be signed (or initialed) by the Recording Secretary or any substitute or secretary pro tem. When a substitute serves as secretary, the President should sign the minutes also.

Essentials of Correct Minutes

It is not necessary to mention all the names of everybody taking part in the meeting. Too many names in the minutes tend toward confusion and add nothing of real value. Only in the case of very important main motions is it advisable to mention the name of the maker of the original motion. The names of seconders are mentioned even less often. Except in very important and debatable motions it is usually quite sufficient to say, "It was moved and seconded."

Names of committee chairmen should be mentioned, however, especially those making reports.

Correct minutes should contain the following facts:

1. The kind of meeting reported, whether regular, special, or adjourned.

2. The name of the organization.

3. Date and place of meeting. (If the organization has a regular or permanent meeting place, the place need not be mentioned unless some change is made and another meeting place used.)

4. The presence of the President or chairman of the meeting, and the Secretary, or in their absence the names of their substitutes.

5. The number or names of members present may be included. (Only in the case of small clubs is it necessary to mention individual names. A fairly accurate estimate of the number of members present, however, is sometimes of value in the minutes.)

6. The statement that the minutes of the previous meeting were read and approved, or that their reading was dispensed with.

7. Reports read and approved. (Details of most reports may be omitted.)

8. Every motion, lost or carried. (Motions withdrawn without vote need not be recorded.)

9. Resolutions, if adopted, must be included in the minutes in full and complete detail. If rejected a complete copy of the resolution is not necessary, merely a statement as to its general purpose.

10. A record of every vote taken by ballot, showing the

number of votes cast on each side of the question. Voting by raising hands, or by standing, should also be recorded by number, but it is not necessary to record numbers in *viva voce* voting.

11. The hour of adjournment.

The outline given above covers only the business meeting. When the business meeting is followed by a "program," whether purely social or part of the outlined plan of club work for the year, the various features of this program must be reported briefly in the minutes.

Example of Correct Minutes

Following is an example of properly constructed minutes, as described above:

JANUARY MEETING—The regular monthly meeting of the Bedford Hills Century Club was held at the home of Mrs. Arthur Smith, Tuesday, January 9th, 1942, with the President in the chair and Miss Neilson acting as Secretary in the absence of Miss Morris. Twenty-two members were present. The minutes of the last meeting were read and approved.

TREASURER'S REPORT—The report of the Treasurer showed that $12.00 in membership dues had been received since the last meeting; $4.30 had been paid out for stationery and postage, leaving a balance in the treasury of $37.75.

STANDING COMMITTEES—Mrs. Croxton, Chairman of the Music Committee, reported that estimates on popular priced concert courses which could be offered to the community at 25 cents a ticket had been received from three concert companies. The Committee had given these estimates careful consideration and recommended that the club present the course offered by The National Music League.

Mrs. Judson moved that the club adopt the recommendation

of the Music Committee and authorize it to take entire charge of the popular priced concert series. Motion seconded. Vote 19 to 3.

Mrs. Kingsley, Chairman of the Resolutions Committee, presented the following resolution:

(*Here follows an exact copy of the resolution.*)

It was moved and seconded that the resolution be adopted. After a brief discussion, the resolution was adopted unanimously.

SPECIAL COMMITTEES—There being no reports from other officers or Standing Committees, the President called for a report from the special committee appointed to work for the installation of a swimming pool in Lincoln Park. Mrs. Raymond, Chairman of the committee, reported that the committee had had interviews with the Superintendent of Parks, Superintendent of Schools, and a committee from the Kiwanis Club, which is interested in the same project, and that estimates as to cost were being prepared by several contracting firms, but the committee is not yet ready to present its recommendations.

DELEGATES TO CONFERENCE ON CAUSE AND CURE OF WAR—The President called attention to the fact that the club had voted at its last meeting to send two delegates to the Conference to be held next month at White Plains on the Cause and Cure of War, and announced that nominations were in order. Mrs. Graham, Mrs. Raymond and Miss Morris were nominated. Since no other nominations were made, the chair declared nominations closed. The chair asked whether the club wished to vote by ballot or *viva voce*. Mrs. Ballard moved that the vote be by ballot. The motion was seconded and carried. The chair appointed Mrs. Lyman and Miss Spear to act as tellers, read the names of the three nominees and instructed members to write two names on each ballot. The tellers reported that Mrs. Graham received 11 votes, Mrs. Raymond 8 votes and Miss

Morris 3 votes. The Chair declared Mrs. Graham and Mrs. Raymond elected delegates.

PROGRAM ON COMMUNITY RECREATION—As there was no further business for the house to consider, the President turned the meeting over to the Chairman of Community Recreation, Mrs. Alfred Hopkins, who presented a program consisting of instrumental music by the High School Orchestra and an address on "Playgrounds or Juvenile Criminals" by Miss Alice Wentworth, of the Playground and Recreation Association of America.

The address was followed by questions and discussion.

After joining in singing "America the Beautiful," the meeting adjourned.

(*Signed*) Lois Burnett (*Secretary pro tem*)
(*Signed*) Elizabeth Wilson, *President*

VIII

How Votes Are Taken and Counted

WE HAVE already mentioned several methods of voting. Let us now consider the subject as a whole. This will involve some repetition of what has been said before, but the subject is so important that it is worthy of a complete presentation.

Voting is the method by which the group expresses its opinion and takes action. It is the voice of the assembly (that is, the members at the meeting), and therefore of the club itself even though the full membership is not present at the time the vote is taken.

It is a general rule that every member who is in the room at the time the question is stated has not only the right to vote, but also the duty. On the other hand, it is equally true that no member can vote who is not in the room at the time the vote is taken. Two exceptions may be made to these statements: first the effect of any members present refraining from voting, and second the possibility of voting by proxy or by mail. These two exceptions will be mentioned later.

Terms Used in Connection with Voting

Let us, at the beginning, define some of the terms used in connection with voting.

PLURALITY—A candidate for office is said to have a "plurality" when he receives more votes than any other candidate. This word has no reference to the total number of members nor to the total number of those present. It has been said that some Presidents of the United States were "minority presidents," i.e., they did not receive a majority of the votes cast in the national election. For example, Woodrow Wilson was a minority president at the time of his first election. He received more votes than any other candidate, but the combined vote for William Howard Taft and for Theodore Roosevelt was greater than that given to Wilson, and would have constituted a majority if they had been centered on one candidate.

MAJORITY—A majority is more than half, but a clear distinction should be made between (1) a majority of the votes cast, (2) a majority of the members present, and (3) a majority of the members. Suppose you have a membership of 50, an attendance of 24, and suppose only 17 of those present vote on a certain question. A majority of the club membership is 26, a majority of those present is 13, but a majority of votes cast is only 9, which, of course, is a small proportion of the total membership (50) and yet under certain circumstances the 9 voters may represent the opinion and action of the entire club membership. Unless otherwise stated in the By-laws, the word "majority" is usually interpreted to mean a majority of the votes cast, not a majority of those present, nor a majority of the total membership.

TWO-THIRDS—When any question requires a "two-thirds vote," this simply means that the affirmative vote must be at least twice as large as the negative vote. The same distinctions apply to the definition of a two-thirds vote as to a majority. A two-thirds vote of the total membership (50) would be 34; two-thirds of those present (24) would be 16, but two-thirds of those voting would be 12. Unless otherwise stated, these 12 voters would represent the necessary two-thirds in this instance.

Most societies do not require a two-thirds vote or even a majority of the total membership, as this might necessitate voting by proxy or by mail, or both.

Methods of Voting

Following are the various methods by which voting is effected:

(1) ACQUIESCENCE—In voting, it may truthfully be said that "silence gives consent." Those who have an opportunity to vote and refrain from doing so must be held to acquiesce in the result of the votes actually cast. When a question is put by the presiding officer, silence or any other method of refraining from voting has the effect of agreeing with the prevailing opinion. There is no method by which these non-voting votes can afterwards be counted or applied to the question at issue, provided that the voters who neglected to use their opportunity were present when the question was put to vote. To refrain from voting does not necessarily mean that you are in favor of the prevailing opinion. It may only mean that you recognize the futility of your opposition and do not wish to go on record or indicate your opinion. If you think the issue is an important one, especially as a matter of principle, you should by all means vote, even if you find yourself in a minority of one.

Another method of silent voting is called "General Consent." If the question at issue is a simple one, a detail and not a matter of principle, and if it may safely be assumed that all present are in agreement, a member may ask for general consent. The Chair repeats the requests and asks if there is any objection. If no objections are expressed, the Chair proceeds in practically the same way as if the matter had been adopted by formal vote. This might be called "voting by silence of the entire assembly." An example of this kind of vote is the usual approval of the minutes. "If there are no objections, the minutes stand as approved" is the customary statement from the chair. After a brief pause, the Chair will say, "The minutes are approved as read."

Other instances where consent by silence is effective and shortens the time consumed in transacting business are the correction of any grammatical errors in motions or resolutions, the correction of spelling or other errors in proper names and similar minutiae. It is taken for granted that consent by silence will not be evoked in any important issue.

(2) VIVA VOCE—Next to acquiescence, or consent by silence, the simplest method of voting is called "viva voce." This is a Latin expression meaning "by voice" or "orally." *Viva voce* voting is simple and quick, and it is possible to dispose of many routine matters in rapid order by this method, but of course it is not effective when applied to controversial questions on which there is a sharp division of opinion. Adoption of reports and other simple motions are usually accomplished by *viva voce*. "All those in favor of accepting the report of the committee will signify by saying 'Aye,' those opposed 'No.' The Ayes have it." This is a common and almost stereotyped form in most meetings for routine business. Sometimes the response comes close to being "consent by silence." If the members are bored with routine and the assembly unresponsive to the chair's efforts to get business done, there may be only a few straggling, half-hearted "Ayes" and no "Noes." But sometimes the viva voce method comes suddenly to life in a startling way. The "Noes" may feel that they are not receiving proper attention and may shout "No" so loudly that it is difficult or impossible to tell which side made the bigger noise. In that case, the chair may decline to announce a decision, and may proceed to repeat the vote by some other method, or some member may demand a second vote on the question by saying, "I call for a

count." Sometimes the expression "division" is used instead of "count," meaning a request for an accurate indication of the way in which the votes are divided. Calling for a count or division by a member of the assembly does not impute any charge of unfairness or prejudice on the part of the presiding officer. It merely means that the member making the call feels that a fair statement of the vote on the basis of the amount of noise made is not possible, or that so many present have failed to vote that a proper expression of opinion is impossible.

Under such circumstances the viva voce vote is not considered to be effective and another method of voting is used, to determine more accurately the sense of the meeting.

(3) SHOW OF HANDS—The Chair says, "All those in favor will signify by raising their right hands." It is important that all those voting keep their hands in the air until they are sure that all have been counted. The presiding officer or the secretary or both count the raised hands and for safety the secretary should write the number down. When all are counted, the Chair asks to have the hands lowered and says, "All opposed please raise their right hands." Again a count is made and then the Chair announces the result of the vote with the number of those voting.

(4) RISING—Another similar method of voting is by rising. The Chair asks all in favor to rise and remain standing until counted. The voters should remain standing until the Chair says, "Be seated." When those opposed have risen and been counted, the result of the vote and the number of those voting is then announced by the Chair.

The method of showing hands and the method of rising are both entirely accurate and dependable if conducted properly, and both methods draw some attention to those present who do not vote. A presiding officer who feels that the assembly is not paying proper attention to the proceedings may endeavor to

wake them up by resorting to either of these methods, preferably voting by rising, even when no "division" is called for from
the floor.

(5) ROLL-CALL—When a motion is considered very important
and the members wish to have a record of the votes cast, a
member may demand a "roll-call." This method of voting is used
only on very serious questions involving important principles. It
is used in Congress on all vital issues. The vote of each Senator
and Representative is recorded as his name is called and this
record may be referred to years later. Few questions in club
life attain the seriousness of justifying a vote by roll-call, but
it is a recognized method of voting and should be called upon
if the occasion seems to warrant its use.

A vote by roll-call is usually asked for by means of a motion,
duly seconded. The Chair says, "It has been moved and
seconded that this vote be taken by roll-call. All in favor say
'Aye,' those opposed 'No.' The Ayes have it. We will vote by
roll-call." It is advisable for the President to reiterate the
question before the house, asking each member in favor of the
main motion to answer "Yes" and each member opposed to
the main motion to answer "No."

The Secretary then calls the roll and each member present
answers "Yes" or "No" as her name is called. Any member
who does not wish to take sides or vote on the question
answers, "Present" and her vote does not count (except for
the underlying principle that "silence gives consent").

After the roll-call, the Secretary reads the names of those
who voted "Yes" and then the names of those who voted "No."
This is to avoid error. If an error has been made, the member
whose vote has been recorded wrongly should immediately
call attention to that fact and have it corrected.

The Secretary then hands the President a paper bearing the

number of votes cast on each side and the President announces the result of the vote, with the numbers voting.

When the vote is taken by roll-call, the Secretary must enter in the minutes the names of each member voting and how the vote was cast. This is a matter of permanent record and may be referred to at any later time.

(6) BALLOT—A method of voting on important matters which is used much more often than the roll-call method is voting by ballot. It is used when absolute accuracy is desired, but when secrecy as to the voting of individual members is also desired. (It is also used when voting by mail.)

Election of officers is usually effected by the ballot method. Acceptance or rejection of proposed new members is also frequently done by ballot, as secrecy is desirable for such action, especially in secret or fraternal organizations where one adverse vote may bar a candidate from membership. As voting by ballot permits a free expression of individual opinion, it is used when opinions on the question at issue differ widely or when the issue may tend to create ill feeling among members.

When voting on a motion or resolution, the ballots are slips of blank paper which are distributed among those present. Each member writes "Yes" or "No," and folds the paper so that the word cannot be seen. The ballots are then collected and handed to a teller or tellers (usually two or in some cases three) who have been appointed by the Chair. If there are two tellers, one has a tally sheet, the other opens the folded ballots and reads off the vote, "Yes" or "No." After all are counted, verification is acomplished by repeating the process with the function of the tellers reversed. The compiler of the tally sheet reads the votes from the ballots and the other teller checks the tally sheet or makes a new one.

The tellers then report the result of the vote to the Chair, who announces the result to the assembly, or the Chair may ask the tellers to make the announcement. The number of votes cast on each side is given with the announcement. The voter's name is written on the ballot and the vote of each member remains a secret.

Election of officers is almost invariably accomplished by ballot. In such elections the names of the candidates for each office are written or printed on the ballots before they are distributed. If a member wishes to vote for a person whose name has not been written or printed on the ballot, she may do so by writing in the new name, although this is not a very satisfactory method. All nominations for office should be made through the regular channels.

Two tellers are ordinarily sufficient to count the ballots, but in large assemblies, especially conventions representing a number of clubs or societies, four tellers are usually appointed.

Some large societies provide a ballot box which is placed in a prominent and accessible position and in which the ballots are deposited, just as in our political elections. The ballots may be inserted in the opening in the top of the box by the voters themselves, or a teller may be appointed to stand by the box and put the ballots in as they are brought up by the voters. When this plan is adopted, it is said that "the polls are open" for the time during which members may deposit their ballots. If the society is in session during the voting, it may close the polls by a two-thirds vote after a reasonable time has been given members to prepare and deposit their ballots. Another method is to declare (by motion and second) that the polls will close at a certain specified hour. This is sometimes worded "the polls will remain open one hour." The polls are then declared open at, let us say, 3 o'clock, and must close promptly at 4. During the elapsed time when the polls are open, the society may conduct any other business which it desires, or may listen to an address or a program. After the polls are closed, no more ballots can be received unless the polls are. re-opened, which can be done by means of a main motion, before the votes are counted.

The tally sheets prepared by the tellers should be signed by all the tellers and turned over to the Recording Secretary as part of the records of the society.

(7) PROXY—Members who are unable to attend a meeting at which important voting is to take place may vote by means of a proxy. A proxy is written and signed authority for some other member (specified in the proxy) to vote for the absent member. Proxies are in common use in business, such as meetings of stockholders, but their use is not so prevalent in club affairs, although it is perfectly legal. It should be a matter of common agreement and arranged for or agreed to in advance. The sudden unexpected appearance of proxies in an important election might lead to unpleasant feelings on the part of the opposition, who might feel that they had not been given an equal chance.

The proxy may be a blank form to be filled in by the voter, or it may be simply an informal note. It should mention the name of the member who is authorized to use it. Sometimes the proxy states specifically the vote to be taken, i.e., the measure to be voted for or against, or the candidate to be voted for or against. Other proxies merely authorize a certain member to vote for the absentee, leaving it to the authorized voter the choice whether to vote for or against.

(8) MAIL—Voting by mail is used only in important matters, such as amending by-laws and electing officers, in organizations whose members are scattered, or when the vote of the entire membership is desired, and not merely the vote of those attending the meeting. Needless to say, whenever voting by mail is resorted to, it is imperative that the entire membership be included, and not merely those who do not expect to attend the meeting. It must be all or none.

(9) CASTING ONE BALLOT—In small informal associations, where the controversial spirit is wholly absent, it is sometimes the custom to "move that the Secretary be instructed to cast one ballot in favor of the candidates nominated," or "in favor of the motion or resolution." In elections this is possible only where one candidate is nominated for each office. It amounts to a unanimous election and is used merely to save time. It is obviously impractical where more than one candidate is nominated for any office, or where any division of opinion may occur or be at all likely to happen. Most parliamentary authorities do not encourage voting by casting one ballot, but it is a custom which persists in a multitude of small friendly groups. If any argument, protest or division of opinion occurs, voting by casting one ballot, like viva voce voting, must give way to a more definite and accurate method.

Under normal circumstances the presiding officer takes no part in the debate on any question and does not vote. The Chair should represent absolute fairness and impartiality. (See page 50.)

When the Presiding Officer May Vote

If the members of the assembly are equally divided and the tally of votes shows a tie, the presiding officer *may* vote, but is not required to. Obviously this is a delicate situation and must be handled with tact. If the members are equally divided, then the question is still controversial, in spite of the fact that a vote has been taken. The Chair, by voting, determines the issue, one way or the other, and this "casting vote" may mean that too high a price has been paid for victory. The impartiality of the Chair may be under suspicion and if the issue is an important one, the wise presiding officer may refrain from voting. In that case, a tie vote means that the motion does not prevail, and the decision is in the negative. This means that further time and thought may be given to the proposition (whatever it is), and at some later meeting the opinions of the members may have clarified and a definite result may be secured when the motion is introduced again.

IX

How Elections Are Conducted

THE ANNUAL ELECTION of officers is one of the most important events of the club year. It usually takes place in the late spring, at the end of the active season, probably in May or June. The meeting is usually a "regular" meeting, that is to say one of the pre-arranged schedule, but it is sometimes called the "annual" meeting. In most clubs and societies it is customary to call attention to the unusual importance of this meeting by means of written notices, mentioning the reading of annual reports and the election of officers.

The date of the election and the list of offices to be filled are determined by the Constitution and By-laws.

The annual election offers an opportunity for the club to give recognition to workers who have shown themselves peculiarly fitted for office by faithful and efficient service and it makes possible the inauguration of new policies when the old ones have proven to be uninteresting or unprogressive.

Methods of Nomination and Election

Nomination and election of officers may be accomplished by one of three methods: (1) from the floor, (2) by committee, (3) by rotation.

Each method has both advantages and disadvantages, and the

method used by your club should be adapted to your own needs and conditions. If the method originally tried out when the club was new does not seem to be satisfactory, another method may be tried only after amending the provisions in the Constitution and By-laws regarding elections. In the Constitution suggested in Chapter III, the annual meeting is designated as occurring in May and it is specified that the election shall be by ballot. The Constitution does not state how the nominations shall be made, but By-law V, Section 2, includes a Nominating Committee as one of the standing committees, implying that the committee method (2) will be used. The Nominating Committee need not be a standing committee. It may be a special committee appointed by the President at some time prior to the election.

As a rule, club members have opinions in regard to the officers well in advance of the annual meeting, and a certain amount of more or less informal discussion is almost certain to take place. A popular president will be re-elected for a second term, or a vice-president who has shown ability will be advanced to the presidency.

Advocates of nominations from the floor (method 1) claim that nomination by committee savors too much of "steam roller" tactics, especially if the Nominating Committee is appointed by the President just before the election. The committee members may prepare a slate without regard to the wishes of the club membership, thus perpetuating in office one group or faction. This is especially true where only one candidate is nominated for each office. Sometimes the President sidetracks the ambitions of an active rival by appointing her a member of the nominating committee, thereby making it impractical for her to nominate herself.

On the other hand, nominations from the floor may be criticized. The friends of one candidate may do a little campaigning in advance of the meeting and catch their adversaries unprepared. There is bound to be a certain amount of self-consciousness on the part of both nominators and nominees when the "from the floor" method is used, and a frank expression is almost impossible. Another objection to nominations from the floor is for exactly opposite reasons to the first one mentioned, for instead of pre-arranged campaigns in favor of one candidate at the expense of others, we may find nominations made hastily and thoughtlessly in cases where a little preliminary consideration might have brought out more capable candidates.

The committee method has one great advantage, as it allows for nominations from the floor in addition to those proposed by the committee. Members sometimes hesitate to avail themselves of this privilege for fear of wounding the feelings of some fellow-member whose name has been put forward by the committee, but when the office is sufficiently important and the difference of opinion sufficiently strong, nomination from the floor is a dignified and commendable proceeding. When such a feeling does exist, the dissenting members who wish to object to the slate as presented by the committee should be on guard against a quick motion to close nominations, or to adopt the report of the Nominating Committee. Either of these motions, if passed, elects the slate as proposed by the committee.

All things considered, nomination by committee is probably the best method and it is used by most organizations.

Following the election of officers, after the result has been announced, it frequently happens that a member will rise and say, "I move that the vote be made unanimous." If the motion has a second, the Chair puts the question and the house votes (usually viva voce) affirmatively, with no dissenting voices. This is merely an act of courtesy in a club where good feeling prevails and it enables the new officers to assume their duties with a feeling of complete co-operation from their membership.

The election of officers in May or June, which is customary in most clubs, is for the purpose of allowing them time to prepare their plans and programs before the next season's work begins. In some organizations the newly-elected officers take office immediately upon election; in other societies they do not assume the offices until the beginning of the active club season, usually September, but in either case the summer months are months of planning.

Following is a description of each of the three methods of voting for election of officers.

(1) FROM THE FLOOR—At the annual meeting, the regular order of business is followed until "New Business" is reached on the agenda. The President then says, "The next business is the election of officers. Nominations for President are now in order."

A member rises and nominates a candidate. Another member (without rising) seconds the nomination. Presumably there will be at least one other nomination and second: possibly three or more candidates may be presented. Each nomination must be seconded or it is not valid.

After a proper pause, the Chair may say, "Are there any more nominations for President?" If there is no response, the Chair says, "The nominations for President are closed," and proceeds to the vote. If the Chair does not act to close nominations, it frequently happens that a member will say, "I move that the nominations for President be closed." This should be done only after a reasonable amount of time, in order to avoid the suspicion of one small group attempting to impose its wishes upon the assembly by limiting a free expression of opinion in the nominations.

According to parliamentary custom, a two-thirds vote is necessary to pass a motion closing nominations. In most cases, it is better for the presiding officer to declare the closing of nominations.

Nominations may be re-opened by a majority vote, before the election has taken place.

These two motions, closing and re-opening nominations may be amended, but may not be debated.

If the Constitution does not provide that officers shall be elected by ballot, any of the methods of voting already described may be used. Where the group is small and friendly and there is little or no rivalry for office, viva voce voting is allowable, especially where only one candidate is nominated for any particular office. Where two or more candidates are under consideration, it is recommended that voting be by means of rising, or by raising the hand, but of course the most satisfactory method and the one most in use is by ballot.

Following the election of President, nominations are made for Vice-President, Secretary, Treasurer, and other officers named in the Constitution; and these officers are elected one by one in the same manner as the President. Where nominations are made from the floor it is usual to elect the officers one by one, as members may be confused by trying to remember so many names and the offices for which they have been nominated. It is possible, though not advisable, to write the names on a blackboard, or for the Secretary to keep a list and prepare ballots after the list is complete, and then the assembly may vote on the ticket or tickets nominated; but the vote by separate office is simpler and more definite.

(2) BY COMMITTEE—In larger organizations and particularly where rivalry for office may exist and members prefer not to make their preferences public, nomination by a committee is the accepted form.

The Nominating Committee may be a Standing Committee which may function for any called-for nominations during the course of the year. During this time also they have an opportunity to observe the various officers and judge their qualifications for office, and when the time comes to make nominations for the annual election, the committee has a background of experience upon which to work.

If the Constitution and By-laws do not establish the Nominating Committee as a Standing Committee, the Chair appoints a special committee and announces it at the meeting previous to the annual meeting. This committee should consist of at least three members, even in a small club, and in a larger club it is advisable to have a Nominating Committee of five or six members.

The ideal Nominating Committee represents the club as a whole and is not composed of any one group or clique within the club. Happy the organization which has no inner groups or cliques, but as time goes on it is almost inevitable that some grouping will occur within the membership. The President may feel that she represents the ruling group and wishes to perpetuate their authority, and in that case will appoint the Nominating Committee from within that group, but this is usually an unhealthy sign and a wise President will avoid any such political alignment if possible.

The Nominating Committee holds a meeting, elects a Chairman, unless the President has already designated the Chairman, and proceeds to work. In many organizations it is customary to nominate only one candidate for each office, except for the Executive Board or Board of Directors or Council. For that group, if three Directors are to be elected, it is customary to nominate five candidates, with instructions to the voters to vote for not more than three. Many societies continue to work together harmoniously and effectively for years with elections at which only one candidate is named for each office, but this indicates an unusual commonness of purpose and friendly co-operation. Even though such a course is possible, you may feel that in the long run it is better to nominate at least two candidates for each office. Any Nominating Committee may, if it chooses, break the tradition of years and make more than one nomination for each office, even though this has never been done before in the history of the club. Whatever is done, the Nominating Committee has an important function to perform and if it acts wisely, it will consult with various officers and members and try to sound out the general feeling within the club membership as to procedure and also as to the popularity of certain individuals.

It is not customary to nominate more than two complete tickets, although the name of a particularly popular member may appear on both tickets, a kind of "fusion" candidate. In making nominations, the Nominating Committee, which should be familiar with the membership and with the history of the club, should consider not only the personal popularity of the proposed candidates, but even more importantly their peculiar fitness for office and the policies which they endorse and the principles for which they stand. Usually the two different tickets represent two different elements in the club membership, the group which is aggressive and radical, and the group which is conservative; or the group which is in favor of cultural programs only and the group which stands for community service. In the choice of President, the personal qualities of the candidate are often more important than the policies represented. Executive ability, outstanding and dynamic personality, ability to speak well in public, or some other personal attribute may be counted on to make a good President, possibly steering a middle course between two extremes of policy represented by the candidates for other offices.

If only one candidate is mentioned for each office, when this report is presented to the meeting by the Chairman of the

Nominating Committee, a motion to adopt the report is equivalent to a motion to elect the candidates mentioned. If any further nominations are to be made from the floor, they must be made before the report is adopted.

If two or more tickets are presented in the report of the Committee, choices must be made by vote, preferably (as has been described) by ballot. No matter how many candidates are proposed by the Committee, further nominations from the floor are always possible, and must be properly seconded. When nominations are made from the the floor, the names of the candidates so nominated must be added to those proposed by the committee. Members should be reminded of this by the presiding officer when the ballots are passed out.

The best form of ballot is a printed one, prepared in advance after the Nominating Committee has made its decisions. In some societies this printed ballot is sent out to the entire membership along with the notice of the annual meeting, thus giving the members ample opportunity to think over the various nominations and decide whether or not to make further nominations.

If printed ballots are not practicable, typewritten ballots may be easily prepared. A sufficient number can be prepared quickly with carbon sheets and reasonably thin paper.

If neither printed nor typed ballots are provided, the names of the candidates should be listed where members can see them easily, on a blackboard or a large cardboard or poster. Blank pieces of paper of sufficient size may then be used as ballots.

Whatever method is used, it is of great importance that the names of candidates nominated from the floor at the meeting should be placed prominently before the membership, so that they will not be at a disadvantage in comparison with the candidates who received nomination from the committee.

(3) ROTATION—This is a method of electing officers which is possible only in very small and closely-knit groups. We some-

times hear of "rotation in office," by which is meant something different from election by rotation. Rotation in office means merely that many clubs do not consider it healthy for the organization to keep certain individuals in the same office for too long a time. A time-limit is fixed, either by By-law or by custom. It may be stated that no officer may be elected to the same office for more than two consecutive terms. She may be elected to some other office, but not to the same one. After the lapse of one term, however, she may be elected again to the office which she filled before.

Election by rotation means that when election time comes around, each officer advances one step. The treasurer becomes secretary, the secretary becomes vice-president and the vice-president becomes president. The president advances one step by retiring from office. Only one new officer has to be elected every year,—the treasurer. Beginning as treasurer, each official may look forward to an official life of four years, one year in each position.

It is obvious that election by rotation is not practical for large and active organizations. It is useful only where there is no possibility of friction or jealousy among the members of the club and no striving for official position.

One advantage of the rotation method for the small club is that the officers prepare for their new duties as they go along. The treasurer learns how to act as secretary while she is discharging her duties as treasurer.

Of course it is most important to make careful selection of the one officer to be elected each year. A person who has never held office may seem like promising material when elected but as time goes on may prove unsuited to responsibility and the remainder of the four years may be a trying experience for all concerned. Another disadvantage is that a splendid treasurer may make a mediocre secretary, or a perfect secretary may make a very poor presiding officer and leader. The rotation method may take the perfect secretary from her proper job although perhaps she and the club membership would prefer to keep her there.

After the Election

But no matter by what method your officers are nominated and elected, when the result of the election is announced, congratulations are in order. The retiring president is the first to felicitate her successor, the defeated candidate for any office the first to congratulate her successful rival.

X

How Finances Are Handled

A CLUB, like an individual, should live within its income, and the problem of how to do so and still lead a satisfactory life, is as difficult for the club as for the individual and sometimes more so, for in all organizations it is true that everybody's business is too frequently nobody's business. It is everybody's money which is involved in the finances of the organization and it is everybody's business to see that it is efficiently handled, but not everybody is going to feel this responsibility, nor to agree on how the desired results are to be obtained. There must be a definite financial responsibility placed by the total membership on the shoulders of a certain individual or group, and with that responsibility must go authority.

Treasurer and Finance Committee

In small, informal clubs the Treasurer may be the watch-dog of the treasury. The President and Secretary sign authorizations for expenditure of the club funds and these three officials keep a watchful eye on all proposals to spend money. Any motions or resolutions presented to the club for action involving the spending of money should be weighed against the available funds and, if in the opinions of this *ex-officio* Finance Committee, the proposed expenditures are not advisable, the club membership should be informed of that fact and every effort made to make the expenditures conform with the assets. Very seldom will the membership vote against the strong advice of its officers.

Outside of the smallest and most informal groups, with slight financial resources and little expectation of spending money, by far the best plan is to appoint or elect a Finance Committee as a standing committee, continuing throughout the entire time of that particular administration, considering all aspects of the financial affairs of the club. The reports and recommendations of the Finance Committee are to be taken very seriously by the club and their advice should be final in all questions involving money. The President is *ex-officio* a member of all standing committees, and the Treasurer should also be considered a member of the Finance Committee, and probably also the Secretary. (In some clubs the Recording Secretary, like the President is ex-officio a member of all standing committees. This is determined by the By-laws.) In addition to the three officials mentioned, the Finance Committee should include two or three or even four individuals from the club membership.

The qualifications and duties of the Treasurer have been discussed. (See Chapter IV.)

Necessary Equipment for Treasurer's Work

The equipment necessary for proper conduct of the Treasurer's work depends a great deal on the size of the club and the scope of its activity. A competent Treasurer will know what account books are necessary for proper bookkeeping,—journal, cash-book, and ledger. If your Treasurer is inexperienced and your club is a new one with no records, the advice of a professional accountant should be obtained and followed.

In addition to the necessary account-books, there should be

one or more card-index files. Many club Treasurers keep two card-files, one for members whose dues have been paid, and one for members who are in arrears.

Two items of printed material are necessary for the Treasurer, (1) vouchers for the proper officers to sign when money is to be paid out; and (2) bills for dues from club members, or for other purposes.

The vouchers should be of uniform size for convenience in filing. Each voucher is numbered, and the number of the corresponding check (paying out the required amount) is added to it when used. Following is a sample voucher:

Name of Club
Date
Number of voucher...........

To the Treasurer:
        Pay to ....
$.....................in payment for.......................
Charge to .... (Name of account under which expenditure
               will be listed in club books)
                Signed.........................
                          President
      ....
                          Secretary
    Check No. ....
    Date paid ....

When the payment is made on a bill which has been rendered to the club, the bill should be attached to the voucher when handed to the Treasurer, and the receipted bill should be filed with the voucher.

Bills for dues will probably be the only printed forms necessary, but if it is anticipated that there will be other bills receivable due the club, blank bill-forms may be provided for the Treasurer's use. Bill-forms should contain a blank line for

Treasurer's signature after the bill has been paid. "Received payment" .... is the usual form. This
Treasurer
does away with the necessity of special receipt forms.

Bank Account

The bank account should always be in the name of the club, not that of the Treasurer. Anyone can place money to the credit of such an account, but only authorized persons can withdraw funds so deposited.

The bank will require written authority from the club as to the signature or signatures to be honored on checks. This authority is usually expressed in a motion, passed at a club meeting, and signed by the President and Secretary.

In addition to the signature of the Treasurer, it is well to authorize one or two other officers or individuals to sign checks and to draw money from the bank for the club in times of emergency such as the illness or death of the Treasurer. The second signer should be the President or Secretary, or Chairman of the Finance Committee, and this second signature must be authorized by the club, proof submitted to the bank in writing and the required signature placed on file with the bank.

The bank which carries the account will also supply the needed check-book (sometimes with the name of the club printed on the checks) and will prepare and send to the Treasurer monthly statements of receipts and expenditures.

Bills and Receipts

An efficient Treasurer sends out all bills for dues at least thirty days before they are payable and these should be followed, when past due, by courteous reminders sent at regular intervals.

All receipt of money should be acknowledged promptly, especially payment of dues. For her own sake, if for no other reason, the Treasurer should keep all records strictly up to date.

All bills should be paid immediately after payment has been authorized. This simplifies bookkeeping, as it is unnecessary and cumbersome to carry an account of "bills payable," in addition to the unavoidable "bills receivable," most of the latter being unpaid dues. Prompt payment of bills also helps to keep up the club credit and standing in the community.

Treasurer's Report

The Treasurer should keep the club accounts in such condition that a detailed statement may be made at any time when called for, although such a detailed statement is not ordinarily made until after the books have been audited, annually or semi-annually. The customary monthly report of the Treasurer, read at regular meetings of the club, is condensed, showing only (1) balance at time of last report; (2) receipts (condensed, not detailed); (3) expenditures (condensed, not detailed); (4) balance on hand.

The annual report of the Treasurer should not be submitted to the club until after it has been audited and certified. If possible it should be printed or mimeographed, and distributed, so that each member may have a copy which can be studied in detail. Typewritten copies, using carbon paper for the necessary number, should be used if printing or mimeographing is impractical. When each member of the club has an opportunity to study at leisure the annual report of the Treasurer, the result is not only a better understanding of club finances, but also a greater interest in the problems involved, and this in turn may stimulate favorable action if and when an appeal is made for more funds.

Special Funds

There is no justification for idle funds. All money not needed for current expenses, (unless donated to a charity or special cause), should be earning interest. It should be put in a savings bank, or invested. Such action should be sanctioned by the club after being recommended by the Finance Committee.

All special funds should be so designated and kept in separate accounts, either at the regular bank, or at another. Under no circumstances should special funds remain in the regular checking account from which funds are drawn for current expenses. If the special funds are expected to remain in the bank for any length of time exceeding three months (such funds for instance as Building funds), they should be placed in a savings bank where they will accumulate interest.

Correct Signature

The correct signature (for business purposes) of a married woman is her own given name. At the bank, she is Jane Doe, not Mrs. John Doe. Titles such as Mrs., Dr., Prof., etc., are not proper on checks, either as payee or signer.

Legal Receipt

Although a cancelled check is considered a legal receipt for a paid bill, in club affairs it is much better to send and to receive receipts for all money transactions. This keeps the records complete and easily verified.

Audit

The accounts of the club should be audited not less than once a year, preferably every six months. Where the treasury has been active, paying out and receiving a large number of items, and where the total amount involved is fairly large, the audit should be done by a professional accountant or auditor. The expense of a professional audit is not a large one, the result is satisfying to all concerned, and the Treasurer and the club membership frequently receive from the professional accountant valuable information in regard to finances and advice as to bookkeeping and the handling of funds.

Where a professional auditor is not employed, at least two Auditors should be appointed or elected from the club membership. They are usually included in the list of officers elected at the annual meeting and although they are not active throughout the year but only at certain specified intervals, they are regarded as officers of the club.

The Auditors need not have had business experience, although it will be helpful if they have had some first-hand contact with some kind of business. The method of the audit is simple and can be accomplished without undue labor in clubs where the accounts are neither complicated nor long.

The Auditors check the cancelled checks with the monthly bank statements and the Treasurer's check-book and cash-account. The vouchers are checked numerically, to see that no number is omitted or duplicated. The checks are also put in numerical order, for the same purpose. The amount specified on each voucher is compared with the amount on the corresponding check. If every voucher is accompanied by a proper check, and if no check is found unsupported by a proper voucher, then the expenditure of funds has been properly accomplished. The Auditors will watch the vouchers carefully to see that they are all properly signed. It may safely be assumed that the bank has kept an equally watchful eye on the proper signing of all the checks which it has honored.

If the vouchers and cancelled checks agree, and if the Treasurer's check-stubs and the bank's monthly statements agree, the Auditors may certify the correctness of the procedure. It only remains to see that the results are properly stated in the Treasurer's report to the membership.

Budget

For any club except the smallest and most informal, the only proper and satisfactory way to handle finances is by means of a budget. When the proposed budget for the coming year is prepared by the Finance Committee, it should be typed, mimeographed, or printed. The stimulating effect of handing each member a copy of the Treasurer's annual report, of which we have made mention, is exceeded by the aroused interest which comes when each member receives a copy of the budget. Plenty of time should be given the members to read and ponder these two vitally important sheets of paper.

If there is no written-out budget (or none at all), the club funds are at the mercy of impulsive and ill-considered motions. Most club memberships are inclined to be overly optimistic in regard to the elastic possibilities of their treasury and a check-rein is usually necessary. Without a budget, it is difficult to hold the club to any definite line of activity, but with certain amounts ear-marked in the budget for expenditure in certain directions, the continuity of effort necessary for the accomplishment of anything worth while is more easily obtained.

A little straight thinking by all the membership in regard to club activities in relationship to club resources is good not only for the finances but for the healthy growth of the definite projects to which the club is committed. If the budget shows an unappropriated balance, the club may then consider what activities it will select in which to use its remaining funds. Also, when the membership fully realizes how much it wishes to do, and how small its margin in dollars and cents, it will face more willingly and more intelligently the problem of either reducing its usefulness or enlarging its resources. Consideration of the budget by club members also tends to cut down disappointment about the uses to which dues are put. When members know where their money has gone (Treasurer's report) and can have a hand in planning where it is to go in the future (budget) they will be better club members.

For a new club, entering on its first year's work, the preparation of a budget must be largely tentative. Expenses can only be estimated and then an effort made to conform as closely as possible to the outlay as planned.

But for a club in its second year or more, the preparation of the budget must be founded upon past experience. In either case, the planning of the budget should begin at least two or three months from the date set for the meeting (presumably the annual meeting) at which the budget will be presented to the membership, discussed, amended, and adopted or rejected.

As a first step, the Treasurer should assemble the records of her predecessors and study and analyze them. If they have been kept accurately and set down clearly, it will not be difficult to ascertain the amounts expended in previous years by various committees and by the club as a whole. When the Treasurer has thus obtained a clear understanding of the club's activities, both past and present, a meeting of the Executive Committee or Board of Directors should be called, at which some idea of the scope of work to be undertaken for the coming year is outlined. These plans are merely tentative, and are used as a basis of discussion. The Chairman of each standing committee and the chairmen of any special committees whose work will carry over into the coming year should be called to this or to a separate meeting and informed in advance, that they should bring to this meeting a statement of the sum which the committee considers necessary for carrying on the work during the coming year.

It will be seen that several meetings will be necessary and a number of informal discussions must take place before anything like an accurate budget can be drawn up. When all the estimates are in hand from the various committee chairmen and others involved, the Budget Committee must consider them in the light of past experience, and decide whether each item should be increased or decreased, must weigh them against other proposed items of expenditure and decide on their relative merits in proportion to the total budget, and above all must consider the certain and the probable income from all sources and keep the budget well within those figures.

Careful budget-makers will insist that the budget remain within the boundaries of the assured income of the club, leaving nothing to chance and incurring no debts or obligations of any kind. This may curtail somewhat the enthusiastic ideas of some members, but in the long run will prove a wise course.

SOURCES OF INCOME. Club money comes from three main sources: dues, assessments, and special money-raising activities. Any possible income from interest on savings-bank accounts or investments may be counted upon as "certain" if the money is already in the bank or invested, but the amounts involved are usually small and good financial policy usually dictates that they be left at compound interest against the proverbial rainy day, and not be used for current expenses.

In budget planning, dues should be depended upon to cover current expenses; assessments should be resorted to only for emergencies or definitely planned expansion of activities; money-raising campaigns should be called upon for special projects.

DUES. The first source of income, dues, is something which can be defined with a fair degree of accuracy. The amount of the annual dues is set forth in the By-laws, in accordance with the requirements of the club and the ability of its members to pay. In the beginning, dues are usually rather too small than too large. As the club grows in size, activity, and prestige, the dues are usually raised. Experience has often proved that the newly-organized club makes a rather timid estimate of what its annual dues shall be, and soon finds that the revenue from this source falls far short of requirements. Suggestion for an advance in the dues is often met with opposition and a fear that it may drive out some old members and discourage new members, but again the experience of many clubs indicates that members think more highly of their club after the dues have been raised and new members are more anxious to join than they were before. One reason for this is that the increased revenue from dues enables the club to develop its former activities and to inaugurate new ones, to carry on with greater dignity and increased prestige, to take a more important place in local and community life. Nothing succeeds like success, and sometimes an era of successful growth and development is ushered in by an increase of dues.

ASSESSMENTS. The second source of income, assessments, should be called upon only in the case of real need. It would be foolish to plan a budget which depended upon assessments for a large part of its financial support. An assessment, or demand for money over and above the dues may be a serious strain on the personal budget of the individual upon whom the demand is made. Even when the money is paid, it is often done grudgingly, and at a personal sacrifice. Other members are annoyed at the mismanagement and apparent lack of fore-thought which made the assessment necessary.

Very often the assessments which cause so much trouble and ill-feeling are not really as necessary as they appear to be. To be sure there are apt to be emergencies which call for funds which may be provided by an assessment, but there are two ways of avoiding this dilemma; one way is by providing an emergency fund kept in a savings bank at compound interest, and the other is to meet the financial demands of the emergency not by an assessment but by a money-raising activity, such as a benefit concert or entertainment, a ball or formal dance, a style show, a block party or any one of the many such events by which money is raised for all sorts of charities and worthy causes. However, if an assessment is called for and seems unavoidable, the only fair thing to do is to bring it up at a regular meeting of the club, present it as a motion, discuss it thoroughly, and then vote on it by ballot. The secret ballot makes it possible for every member to express a free and definite opinion without personal prejudice. If the result of the ballot shows that a large number of members are opposed to the assessment, then it should be abandoned, even if this means disappointment to many. The ill-feeling engendered by an unpopular assessment often rankles for a long time. If assessments are resorted to at intervals which the membership feel are too frequent and for causes which do not seem to require such drastic treatment, in other words if the club continually lives beyond its real income, then a thorough-going study and analysis of the whole financial situation is called for, and the club and its officers must learn to live within the club income. This means one of two things, either raising the dues, or cutting down the expenses. The following remedy for financial ills was once recommended to a club by a financial expert who was called in from the outside to advise the club as to how it could avoid constantly recurring deficits. After listening patiently for a long time and asking a few pertinent questions, the expert quietly rose, picked up his hat and said, "I think your whole financial sub-structure needs to be re-studied." After his departure the club members gave long and anxious thought as to the meaning of his words, then abandoned the assessment plan forever, and raised the dues.

MONEY-RAISING PROJECTS. The third method of raising money, which we have already mentioned, has the advantage of bringing the club members together in congenial work for a common purpose and also frequently brings the club prominently before the community and increases its prestige. Before embarking on a money-raising project, consider carefully some of the questions involved: Will the project really bring in a profit if successful? Are you sure you can make it successful? If it is a plan involving the community, such as a concert, pageant, or dramatic performance, in addition to insuring a successful performance, you must also consider if the entertainment is of a character to appeal to your community, if you can count on the enthusiastic co-operation of the entire club membership to sell tickets in advance, thus avoiding financial disaster on account of an unexpected rain or snow storm on the night of the performance, and if the price of admission is high enough to pay your expected profit and at the same time low enough to bring a crowd into the hall as well as money into the box office.

On the subject of benefit performances, it is wise to be prepared for the worst, and a guarantee fund should be laid aside or provided by generous members to foot any bills which may not be covered by the income at the box office. This is called "underwriting" the performance and is never neglected by wise clubs when embarking on ambitious benefit performances. Underwriting a performance is like endorsing a promissory note. If all goes well the underwriters will not be called upon, but the underwriting fund or the promissory note should be there in case of unexpected catastrophe so that the burden of debt should not fall upon an inadequate club treasury.

The number of activities which can be put on by clubs with both pleasure and profit is large, one might almost say endless. In addition to those mentioned, almost any kind of a gay party can be turned to the benefit of the club; barn dances, country fairs, flower shows, hobby shows, special suppers and dinners with home-cooked food, masquerade parties of various kinds,— a little imagination will lengthen the list and good judgment on your part will select the right one.

TOTAL ANTICIPATED INCOME. To sum up the sources of income, the wise Budget Committee will base most of their calculations on revenue from dues. Even here they will be wary of over-optimism. It is wise to allow for a possible 5% or 10% loss from non-payment of dues. Also, where a campaign for new members is projected, the Budget Committee will not count the chickens before they are hatched and will allow the anticipated new income to play a very lowly part in the budget.

ANTICIPATED EXPENSES. Having arrived at a fair estimate of the income which may be definitely counted on, the Budget Committee will turn its attention to the necessary expenses, and build from there up. Some basic expenses are unavoidable and cannot very well be reduced. These are mostly to be found in the classification known as "overhead." Stationery, printing, postage—these are "overhead." So also are rent, light and heat, telephone, dues to the national organization or federation to which the club may belong, secretarial help, janitor's service—any expenses of this kind which are basic to the existence of the club and which cannot very well be omitted or reduced are "overhead" and must be included as the first section of the budget.

Next there are other expenses which are nearly as essential as those named, but which *could* be curtailed or omitted if absolutely necessary, such as printing programs for meetings and entertainments, printing menus for luncheons and dinners, providing flowers for guests of honor and for speakers and musicians, purchasing books, magazines and pamphlets for the club library and for the study programs.

A third heading for the budget is "Sundries" or "Miscellaneous," to take care of unforeseen expenses, especially small items which are not easily classified. "Miscellaneous" may cover a multitude of sins and this classification is frequently a headache to conscientious bookkeepers and auditors. It is too fatally easy to tuck away all kinds of expenses into this commodious receptacle. Unless watched carefully and cut down to a minimum, "miscellaneous" may turn out to be a dangerous leak in the budget.

Committee chairmen must be impressed with the seriousness of their obligation to provide the Budget Committee with proper estimates of the anticipated expenses of their various activities. This will stimulate them to prepare their plans as nearly as possible before the beginning of the club year. The Program Committee will ask for a certain amount to pay for special speakers, musicians and entertainers, and possibly railroad fare or cab fare for some of them. Printed programs will be included in that department also. Hospitality is another item which must not be overlooked. Many clubs meet for luncheon, tea, dinner, or a late evening supper. These events may call for some expense for service, even in clubs where the food and drink are furnished by club members. Table decorations are items for the budget, or must be provided by members. If your club contributes to local civic activities, possible charges on the budget must be anticipated, such as prizes offered for essays written by school children, contributions to local charities, and other generous gestures.

All these items, many of them small, should be provided for under proper classification in the budget, and not left for the all-embracing "Miscellaneous."

It should be remembered that all club funds should be deposited in the club account and drawn upon only by the Treasurer (or temporary substitute) upon proper authorization.

The various departments and committees submit their bills to the proper authorities for verification and approval, but the actual paying-out is done by the Treasurer. It is necessary to keep this important function in the hands of one person, otherwise fiscal chaos is almost inevitable.

XI

How Committees Work

COMMITTEES have been called "the eyes and ears" of a club. In many cases they are also its "hands and feet." The proper use of committees enables the club to accomplish a greater quantity of business, by dividing it among the members, than would possibly be accomplished if the whole body were to devote itself to each particular subject. Committees are appointed to obtain information on any subject and to analyze and arrange it so that it can be presented to the club briefly and clearly, and to discuss any specific problem so as to be able to recommend to the assembly what action should be taken.

Committees may not always act for the club itself, but as their findings and recommendations are for the most part followed by the club, in a sense they do act for the membership and their duties and responsibilities are not to be taken lightly.

Types of Committees

Committees are of two kinds: Standing Committees and Special Committees.

Standing Committees are provided for in the By-laws. They are usually created either by appointment or election at the annual meeting or immediately afterward. In most clubs the President appoints the Standing Committees, and they become

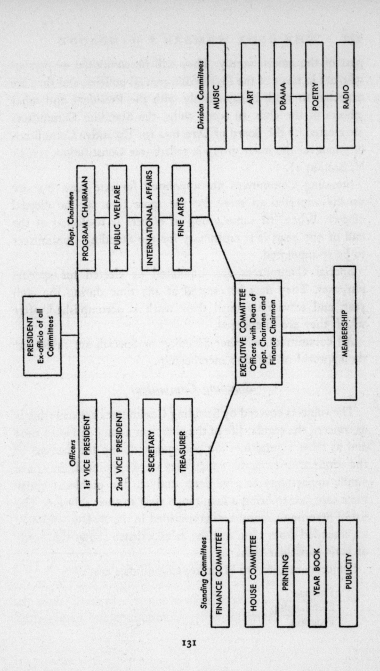

PRESIDENT
Ex-officio of all Committees

Officers
1st VICE PRESIDENT
2nd VICE PRESIDENT
SECRETARY
TREASURER

Dept. Chairmen
PROGRAM CHAIRMAN
PUBLIC WELFARE
INTERNATIONAL AFFAIRS
FINE ARTS

Division Committees
MUSIC
ART
DRAMA
POETRY
RADIO

EXECUTIVE COMMITTEE
Officers with Dean of Dept. Chairmen and Finance Chairman

MEMBERSHIP

Standing Committees
FINANCE COMMITTEE
HOUSE COMMITTEE
PRINTING
YEAR BOOK
PUBLICITY

part of the official family. They will be composed of persons who are in favor of the President's general policies, and they are expected to work harmoniously with the President and other officers of the club. In some clubs, the Standing Committees are elected by the Board of Directors (or Executive Committee, or whatever the inner group is called—see Constitution, Article V, Section 1).

Standing Committees are appointed for one year, but are usually expected to serve for the same term as the elected officers. When the same group of officers is re-elected at the end of one year, it is customary for the Standing Committees to be re-appointed.

Special Committees are appointed or elected for specific purposes. They may be created at any time during the club year, and serve only until their work is accomplished, after which they are discharged.

All committees, whether Standing or Special, are subject to the approval of the club membership.

Standing Committees

The subjects covered by Standing Committees are such things as concern the regular life of the club over a long period of time and as these committees are permanent during the lifetime of the administration under which they were appointed, they have ample opportunity to give deep study to the problems under their care and to bring a long-range view to their solution. The list of Standing Committees is specified in the By-laws and may be amended from time to time as experience shows the needs of your particular club.

Subjects entrusted to Standing Committees are:

> Finance
> Membership
> Program

House (even if you have no clubhouse, a House Committee
is advisable, to look after all details connected with
the meeting place or places)
Nominating (may be a Special Committee if desired)
Resolutions
Hospitality

Other subjects which may be entrusted to Standing Committees are:

Library
Scholarships
Junior Membership
Americanization
Music

Special Committees

During the course of a regular club business meeting, if a subject requires more investigation or discussion than can be given
to it during the course of the meeting, or if more information is
needed than is at that time available, or if it seems advisable
for any other reason, a committee can be appointed or elected
to take the whole matter under consideration and bring back
the required information and recommendations for action at
the next meeting or meetings. This is done by means of a main
motion, which is called a "motion to commit." "I move that the
question be referred to a committee to be appointed by the
Chair, and that the committee be instructed to report at the next
meeting." The motion may also stipulate how many members
the committee should have, or who the chairman is to be, or
may ask that the committee be elected by the assembly and not
appointed by the Chair, and it may also instruct the committee
as to just what its duty is. In some cases the motion gives the
committee "power to act."

If the motion to commit is adopted, then the question under

discussion (whether main motion or resolution together with all pending amendments) is turned over to the committee and no further action taken on it by the assembly, until the committee reports.

Special Committees may be sub-divided into two classes:

(1) *Committees to investigate.* These committees have no power to act for the club. For instance, a committee may be appointed to confer with the committee from another club, or local School Board or Chamber of Commerce in regard to plans for some public improvement, such as a swimming pool in a park. All this committee is expected to do is to gather all the information available as to the possibilities of such a project, the feeling of the community about it, its desirability, its cost and other facts. These facts are reported back to the assembly, with or without recommendations for action.

(2) *Committees to carry out specific projects.* For instance, a committee may be appointed to have full charge of preparing and presenting an entertainment, a concert, or a picnic. This committee has power to act, although its powers may be strictly defined in the motion creating it. Its power to spend money or involve indebtedness may be very definitely limited, or its power to involve the club in any further commitments along the same line. A committee might have power to conduct all the necessary details in connection with putting on a concert, without having power to commit the club to a course of concerts covering a whole season.

Size of Committees

The size of committees is determined by the size of the club and the importance of the subject which they are to consider. As a rule a small committee functions more easily and effectively than a large committee. The whole purpose of the committee method is to bring a subject into sharp focus before a small group rather than the larger assembly. Committees usually consist of three or five members. The uneven numbers are preferred as they make impossible an equal division within the committee.

In addition to the individuals appointed from the membership, the President is usually *ex-officio* (that is, *by reason of office*) member of all committees, so also in some clubs are the Vice-President, Secretary, and Treasurer. This is determined by the By-laws.

Selection of Committee Members

In selecting committee members, it is customary to name those who are known to be interested in the subject under consideration or friendly to the project to be studied. Anyone who is known to be in opposition to the project or who has spoken against it in the assembly is never appointed on the committee to consider that particular subject. This is an unwritten rule of club life. The committee is supposed to be fair-minded and to approach the subject without prejudice, and experience has taught that friendly interest on the part of committee members is more apt to produce a satisfactory result than active opposition.

It sometimes happens, even under the most favorable auspices, that a committee is unable to agree and to render a unanimous report to the club. In that case, the outvoted minority of the committee, if they wish to do so, may submit a "minority" report to the club. This is just for the club's information. The majority report is considered as the report of the committee, and the minority report cannot be discussed or acted upon unless there is a motion to substitute it for the regular committee report. A motion to substitute is not debatable, and must be put to vote without discussion. The club may reject the minority report, or may if it chooses reject both reports and refer the matter back to the committee for further study. In the case of Special Committees, the club may indicate its dissatisfaction by voting to dismiss the committee and create a new one.

The membership of the various committees should include as large a part of the club membership as is possible without making the committees too large and cumbersome. Probably nothing contributes more to club vitality than the inclusion of many members in active committee service, and nothing introduces a new or shy member into the real spirit of the club quite as well as participation in committee work does. On the other hand, nothing is more inimical to the growth of a fine club spirit than the concentration of authority into a few hands and the appointment of the same people on many different committees so that only a small group has any inside working knowledge of the activities of the club and control of its destiny.

While it is true that there are advantages in appointing a large cross-section of the club membership to committee activity, it is also true that committees are of no use unless they do their work. No member should be put on a committee unless she is willing to do her share of the work and take her share of the responsibility. Sometimes the appointment of new and untried members on committees is an experiment which does not produce satisfactory results, but as a matter of principle it is a good method to follow.

Whoever creates the committee, either the chair by appointment or the assembly by election, may at the same time name the chairman. When the committee is appointed by the chair, it is the custom that the first person named shall be chairman of the committee. This is merely a matter of tradition and need not be followed exactly. The first person appointed may not wish to act as chairman, or may not feel qualified to do so, in which case she acts as temporary chairman at the first meeting of the committee, giving way to a permanent chairman. When signing a report, or otherwise appearing in print, it is frequently the custom for the chairman to be named last instead of first. This again is custom, not rule.

Rules for Committee Action

If the work of the committee involves the use of any papers belonging to the club, such as motions, resolutions, letters and other important documents, they are turned over to the chairman of the newly-created committee by the Secretary of the club, and must be returned to the Secretary unmarked after the committee has finished its work. Any changes, alterations, amendments, or eliminations desired by the committee must be written on different sheets of paper and not on the official document.

No one should attend committee meetings except its own members or such persons as the committee may call upon for information or advice.

In minor matters, or when a committee has to act promptly and a meeting cannot immediately be held, the members of the committee may be consulted and may take action by telephone, provided every member is consulted and there are no objections to such a method of expediting business.

Committee meetings may be likened to regular assemblies of the club on a small scale, but when the committee is a small and friendly one, the less formality the better. But no matter how informal and co-operative the committee, it is essential to have at least a chairman and a secretary. The chairman may be elected by the committee in the usual way if none has been appointed. It is not customary to designate a secretary when a committee is appointed. This is usually done by the committee at its first meeting. It is not usually necessary to keep minutes of committee meetings. The duties of the secretary are to make notes of the proceedings and to record the decisions and actions taken. The discussions are not formal, and are "off the record."

It is essential that each committee knows exactly what its job is. This should be stated clearly when the committee is appointed and the chairman should remind the members of their purpose if they show a tendency to wander away from the subject in hand or to encroach upon the province of other committees. On account of the relative intimacy and informality of committee meetings, it is sometimes more difficult to keep the committee in line and at its proper work than to do so with the larger but more formal assembly.

The chairman is responsible for notifying members of the committee as to the date, hour, and place of the meeting; for opening the meeting on time and conducting it in a business-like manner. Parliamentary rules are not enforced, but the chairman should guide the discussion so that the main objects of the committee meeting are accomplished to the satisfaction of all the members. The chairman may express opinions without turning over the chair to another member, and the chairman may join in any votes taken,—thus differing from the procedure at club meetings.

Reports by Committees

The committee's report is compiled from the notes kept by the secretary. The report is usually written by the chairman, and must be agreed to by the members of the committee before being presented to the club. In important reports, involving questions of club policy or the spending of money, it is advisable to have each member of the committee sign the report. In most instances, however, it is sufficient to have the report signed by the chairman only.

Two copies of the report should be made, one to be retained by the chairman of the committee, and one to be handed to the Recording Secretary of the club.

The correct procedure for presenting reports is as follows:

At the proper time in the order of business, the Chair announces, "We will now have reports from Committees. Will the Chairman of the Membership Committee please report?"

The Membership Chairman rises. If she is to read an important report it is customary to step to the front of the assembly or to the platform, but for informal and casual reports it is proper to remain standing. It is a matter of courtesy to address the Chair, "Madam President," and the Chair recognizes the speaker by mentioning her name.

Having read the report, the Chairman hands a copy to the presiding officer or the Recording Secretary (usually the latter), and says, "I move that this report be accepted." As Chairman of the Committee which has done the work and which stands back of the information and advice contained in the report, it is quite proper for the Chairman to move its acceptance. If, for any reason, she fails to do so, the Chair will say, "You have heard the report of the Membership Committee. Will someone make a motion to have it accepted?" or "What is your pleasure?"

If the report contains recommendations for action by the club, the motion is "I move the acceptance of this report and the adoption of its recommendations."

After motion to accept (and adopt) has been made and seconded, the question is then open for discussion and vote.

If a Special Committee has performed signal service for the

club or community, or if its labors have been particularly difficult, a vote of thanks may be passed when the report is accepted.
(It should be remembered that the Special Committee is automatically dissolved after the acceptance of its final report.)

If a Special Committee is not yet ready to report, the Chairman rises and states this fact, asking that the Committee be
given more time.

Standing Committees need not be called upon for reports at
every meeting. The presiding officer should inform herself in
advance of the meeting as to which Standing Committees may
be expected to have reports, and which not. If a Standing Committee is not prepared with a report when called upon, the
Chairman may rise and say, "This Committee has no report
to make."

It is not necessary to vote upon a committee report containing
no recommendations for action, but it is customary to make
some gesture of acceptance. The Chair may say, "If there are
no objections, the report is accepted as read."

Acceptance of reports is frequently very perfunctory. Perhaps
the members have not listened very attentively to the report.
At its conclusion someone says "I move the report be accepted."
Seconded. "All those in favor say Aye, opposed No. The report
is accepted." It is all very casual, but this off-hand manner of
treating committee reports may lead to trouble. Remember
that a committee report which contains a recommendation for
action, when accepted, commits the club to that course of
action. Listen carefully to reports, and vote intelligently on
them.

Another fact to keep in mind concerning committee work is
that no question, whether motion or resolution, can be discussed, voted upon, or considered in any way by the assembly
while it is in the hands of a committee. If you have appointed
a committee to work on that project for a swimming pool in

the public park, then the swimming pool is not to be discussed nor any action taken in regard to the plan until the committee has made a report.

This rule does not apply to Standing Committees unless they are considering some special project or problem. The existence of a Finance Committee does not mean that finances cannot be discussed, but if the question of raising extra funds in order to participate in a Community Christmas Tree pageant has been referred to the Finance Committee, then that particular plan is not a subject for debate until after the report of the Finance Committee is before the assembly.

Committee of the Whole

The "Committee of the Whole" is a parliamentary device for use in large and rather formal assemblies when a more informal discussion is desired than can be obtained under strict laws of debate. The whole assembly resolves itself into a committee, and for the time being the regular order of business of the meeting is in abeyance until the particular problem under consideration is worked out. The presiding officer asks some member of the assembly to take the chair and takes her place with the other members of the assembly. Rules as to the length of speeches and the number of speeches which can be made by any individual are temporarily suspended and the debate is carried on with the freedom which prevails at committee meetings. In order to transform itself into a Committee of the Whole, the assembly must hear a motion and second to that effect and must vote on it.

The Committee of the Whole is an unusual procedure in club life, as most clubs conduct their discussions with considerable freedom and so do not feel the need of a relaxation of the rules of debate.

XII

How Correspondence Is Conducted

NOTHING defines the status of a club in the minds of outsiders more clearly than the manner in which its correspondence is handled. Letters to other organizations, business and professional men and women, speakers and artists, reveal the business and social standing of the club, the efficiency or inefficiency of its officers, and the general character of its members.

Two factors must be considered in handling club correspondence, first the stationery, and second (even more important) the phrasing and meaning of the letters themselves.

Necessary Equipment

With printed stationery done so much better nowadays than it used to be, at comparatively small expense, there is no reason why even small clubs should not have their own letterhead. Very good letterheads with envelopes to match can be had for a price little larger than that of a good grade of unprinted stationery, and the improved appearance of the club's correspondence, with a corresponding increase in dignity and prestige, is certainly worth the slight additional expense.

Correspondence cards to be used in writing notes and other informal communications may be added to the regular letter-size or note-size stationery. A good imitation of engraving is now used by many clubs which wish to have a special superior grade of stationery at a cost considerably less than real engraving. In choosing cards and letterheads, unusual and freakish sizes and shapes should be avoided, and conservative color combinations are always in good taste.

White or cream-colored stationery stamped with black or dark blue is preferable to brighter colors or more subtle shades. The regular sizes for paper and envelopes are to be recommended. For one thing they are cheaper, being regulated not by club custom but by economy in cutting paper at the factory or printer's shop.

The envelope should always conform to the size, shape, and color of the paper, and should be of the same grade. The name and address of the club, or of the sender, should be printed on the envelope, preferably on the flap.

For a small club, with no expectation of an extended correspondence, it is economical to print on the stationery only the name of the club. If you have a club house or meeting place where mail is received, this may be added, but if the replies to club letters are to be sent to individual homes, the address of the club should be omitted. The advantage of printing only the name of the club is that when there is a change of officers, the stationery is still good, otherwise with every change of officers your stationery becomes obsolete. When names of officers are mentioned on the stationery, care should be taken to order a quantity which shall not greatly exceed the anticipated use.

If any names are used on club stationery, club custom is that the name of the President shall appear on all stationery. Next in order is the name and address of the Corresponding Secretary. The name and address of the Treasurer may be printed on a special allotment of stationery for that official, or the name of the Treasurer may be added to that of the President and Corresponding Secretary, making three names in all.

Some organizations go beyond this three-name stationery and print the entire list of officers, running down one side of the page. This can only be done on letter-size paper, and even then it frequently results in limiting the amount of blank space to an uncomfortable degree. When the full list is used, it is not customary to give the address of each officer. The address of the club itself (if any) and the addresses of the three officers mentioned, should always be given if they are to use the stationery.

When the club has a house of its own, or a permanent meeting place which is frequented by members outside of meetings, stationery for members' use may be provided, just as a hotel provides stationery for guests. This is called "house stationery," and is stamped only with the name and address of the club. House stationery is usually note size rather than letter size and is usually more personal in character rather than business-like, to avoid giving the impression that letters written on it are official communications from the club itself.

It is an advantage if all letters coming officially from the club, through its officers, can be typewritten, especially those which concern business matters and official actions of the club, such as motions and resolutions. This applies even to official resolutions of condolence, though more personal notes of condolence and congratulation may be hand-written. Carbon copies of all typewritten letters should be kept for filing. When the letters are hand-written, a copy should be kept for the file, or at least a notation of the contents of the letter.

Conducting Club Correspondence

Club correspondence naturally is handled chiefly by the Corresponding Secretary. She conducts all correspondence dealing with business upon which the club has acted; all letters or notes of sympathy, condolence, or felicitation voted by the club. In forwarding motions and resolutions voted by the club concerning outside affairs or individuals, she must be absolutely accurate as to wording and form. She also handles all official mail with any state, district, or national organization with which the club may be affiliated.

The President usually writes invitations to guests of honor for meetings, luncheons, banquets, and conventions; she answers all similar invitations which she may receive; and she writes personal notes of courtesy to members of the club or affiliated associations, especially when a death occurs.

The Treasurer handles all correspondence bearing upon the club's finances, polite notes or reminders to delinquent members and all persons outside the club who may owe the organization money. If there are pledges of financial support from non-members, communications to them are usually signed by the Treasurer.

Chairmen of Standing or Special Committees correspond with other chairmen who are doing work of a similar kind.

The Chairman of Program writes all letters to speakers and musical artists in or out of town, except an occasional letter which may be written by the President to an especially distinguished guest or someone to whom the club wishes to pay a special courtesy. Specific information should be given to speakers and guests as to date, hour, and place of meeting, the speaker's place on the program, and the arrangements for meeting him and transporting him to the auditorium or place of meeting.

This last item is so important, especially if there is a lengthy list of speakers who are to be heard during the course of the club season, that some clubs create a Standing Committee on Transportation. The Transportation Chairman will in that case take over these duties, writing to the visiting artist or speaker about railway, bus or other transportation, enclosing time tables and stating who will meet the guest at the station.

There may also be a Chairman of Hospitality to arrange for hotel accommodations during a convention, a task which will involve a certain amount of correspondence.

The Chairman of Press and Publicity conducts all correspondence with local papers, as well as statements to any publications of state or national circulation publishing news of such organizations. To the local press should be sent press stories as to coming events, accounts of meetings, and other forms of club news for which there is public interest. The Chairman of this committee may also have occasion to write to the papers correcting erroneous statements which may have appeared, especially concerning resolutions or other official acts of the club.

Good Form in Club Correspondence

The name and address of the person, firm, or organization to which the letter is written should always appear, either at the beginning of the letter, or at the bottom of the page, on the left-hand side. Following the name and address, the "salutation" should be "Dear Sir" or "Dear Madam." The use of proper names should be confined to cases where the recipient of the letter is already established on a personal, friendly basis with the club. When the letter is sent to a business firm, or to another club or committee, when the recipients are men, the salutation is "Dear Sirs," or "Gentlemen." When the club or committee is composed of women, there is no method of salutation which is commonly accepted. This lack of traditional custom is probably due to the fact that women have taken an active part in public and community life so comparatively recently that no form of procedure has been firmly established. You may say "Ladies," (corresponding to "Gentlemen"), or some people prefer the plural of "Madam,"—"Mesdames." We have taken this word over from the French, and while it is familiar to us in the singular, it has an exotic tinge when used in the plural. If you do not wish to be a pioneer in this field, you can usually avoid the awkward phraseology by addressing your letter to the Chairman or head of the group and fall back on "Dear Madam."

Like the salutation, the closing of the letter should be courteous but leaning to the formal and impersonal rather than to the informal, more intimate manner. The good old non-committal "Yours truly" is the best, but "Yours very truly" or "Sincerely yours" may be used if desired, although they add nothing to the simpler form. In friendly greetings between clubs, "Cordially yours" is acceptable.

It need hardly be said that personal letters should not be written on official club stationery, except of course the house stationery already mentioned. Officers and chairmen of committees should be particularly careful not to express on official stationery any personal opinions in regard to club matters or public affairs which may come before the club for discussion, especially where these matters are controversial.

If the address of the official writing the letter is not printed on the stationery, it should be typed or written legibly under the personal signature, which may be partially illegible. If the writer is a woman, this custom informs the recipient of the letter whether the officer should be addressed as "Miss" or "Mrs." A married woman signs her letter by hand thus:

Elizabeth Holden,

and under this signature she writes or types:

Mrs. George Henry Holden, President.

General Suggestions Concerning Correspondence

If you have occasion to write a letter in the name of your club, remember that you are speaking not only for yourself but for a group, and try to make your letter as accurate an expression of the group as you can. This does not mean that it should be stilted, or expressed in formal terms. Writers often cramp their natural spontaneous expression by trying to follow some conventional phraseology, or trying to imitate a predecessor or some other official whose manner of expression may be quite different. A well-written letter should be like a well-spoken statement.

Unless you are an experienced club officer (and perhaps even if you are), it is best to plan your letter before putting anything down on paper. Your letter is an official document belonging to the club, and it may be referred to in an important issue at some time in the future when you have quite probably forgotten just what you did say.

What is the essential message you wish to convey? It should be stated concisely, but completely. If your reader is not familiar with the subject, it must be explained briefly. Is your letter intended to be persuasive, or is it merely informative, or is it an inquiry? In the two latter cases, you should state your message quickly, using short, crisp sentences. If you wish to be persuasive, it will take a little more time, as abruptness may be business-like, but it is seldom persuasive. If you are asking a favor in the name of the club, consider carefully the probable reaction of the recipient.

Ask yourself, would you like to receive a letter phrased in such a manner?

If you are doubtful of just how you want to phrase the letter, prepare an outline or skeleton of what you wish to say, sketch in the most important sentences and, for a final test, write the whole letter and read it aloud, either to yourself or to some one who is willing to give a listening ear and a little advice. Above all, avoid repetition.

XIII

How Programs Are Conducted

IN CLUB PARLANCE, "Program" means that part of the meetings which is not concerned with the transaction of business. "Program" may mean a purely social affair, a "get together," or a serious lecture on an important subject: it may mean an entertainment the sole purpose of which is to amuse the guests, or a debate on some controversial problem of the day. "Program" also is used to mean action along some definite lines, such as civic betterment. The business meetings carry on the work of the club itself and are conducted according to parliamentary law; the character of the program is determined solely by the purpose and scope of the club.

Selection of Program Committee

It is obvious that the Program Committee is one of the most important groups within the club. Its personnel should be selected with unusual care and it should be appointed or elected in ample time to be able to devote plenty of time to formulating the program for the coming year. In some clubs, with diversified interests, the Program Committee is appointed six months before the beginning of the club year.

Powers and Responsibilities of Program Committee

Probably a club's success depends more upon the wise planning of programs than upon any one other single factor. This is especially true of the small club whose program for the year must be sufficiently varied to be enjoyed by a group of members who are interested in a wide range of subjects.

Clubs organized for the study of one definite, specific subject such as art, music, literature, home economics, civics, international relations, base their study outline on this topic exclusively, enlivening the meetings with an occasional social gathering or musical program.

Larger clubs, whose membership runs 200 or more, usually form departments, such as fine arts, education, civics, etc. Members enroll for departments in which they are interested.

The small club organized for no specific purpose other than friendly co-operation along purely cultural lines, with no objective of practical action in view, should make a survey of what its members like best and should plan a diversified program, touching as many interests as is consistent with an adequate presentation of each. This means that, for a few years at least, it will not make an intensive study of any one subject. There are hundreds of successful clubs of this character all over the country, both among men and women, many of them including both men and women. This is particularly true in the arts, and many of the social-cultural clubs meet for lunch or dinner at regular intervals. Their organization is simple and their business is conducted in brief sessions, most of the time being given over to the "program," which ranges all the way from the conventional after-dinner speech to addresses by important individuals, debates, and entertainment.

Many clubs which start out with such a simple plan develop

with the passing of time into more extensive and varied programs, where the discussion of important issues results in
definite and practical action. Also many clubs which begin with
a wide extent and variety of interests, gradually settle down to
one or two definite topics on which they concentrate their
interest and efforts.

In small communities the club must often serve both intellectual and social interests. In rural communities, where
members must travel a considerable distance, many clubs plan
their regular meetings so as to get the most out of them both
socially and intellectually. The members gather at 11 o'clock,
conduct the business meeting with dispatch, follow this with a
program of music and papers by club members. Luncheon is
provided by a hard-working committee, or may be a "basket
lunch," where each member provides his own food. After lunch
may come a debate on the papers read at the morning session, or
a speech by some individual prominent in politics, economics,
or other public affairs. The meeting disbands about the middle
of the afternoon. Some of these "clubs days" are held in private
homes, members acting in turn as hostesses, or the meeting
place may be a Grange Hall, Community House, or church
parlor.

When the club has a diversity of interests and the Program
Committee has to choose the subjects as well as to decide how
they shall be treated, it is wise to consult the membership,
either formally at a meeting, or by means of informal conversations, for the success or failure of the program may depend largely
upon a complete co-operation between the Committee and the
membership. Informal discussion is usually best, but some clubs
make the program for the coming year a matter of debate,
and instruct the Program Committee by vote as to what subjects they wish to study and how they wish to do it.

The Program Committee should also have a clear idea of how

deeply the membership wishes to go into the subject or subjects included in the program for the year, whether they wish to do some research themselves, or to depend entirely upon outside speakers, whether they wish to make a serious study or will be satisfied with a superficial approach.

Whether the Program Committee is left to its own judgment, or definitely instructed by the club, it should in any case have absolute authority. A competent Committee will exercise this authority with tact and discretion. There may be some subject in which the Committee members are tremendously interested, but which, they may discover, is not at all popular with other members of the club. In that case, the Committee will probably drop that subject, or treat it merely as an unessential detail of the whole program, even though theoretically they have absolute authority, and could force the subject on the club if they chose to do so. Once the decisions of the Committee have been made, the program for the year settled upon and dates with outside speakers arranged for, there must be no serious criticism from the club nor any effort to change the program in mid-season. You have given the Committee the responsibility of drawing up the program; they have acted in good faith and to the best of their ability; and that is the end of it. It would be impossible for any Program Committee to prepare a satisfactory program under any other circumstances.

Subjects for Programs

For clubs which are not devoted to one subject or activity, but which wish to study a wide variety of topics, the range of possibility is so great that it constitutes a dangerous temptation to spread the club program so thin that it leaves no worth-while deposit in the minds of the members after the year is over. A Program Committee that ranges high, wide, and handsome over the whole of history and art, with a few deft touches of politics thrown in here and there, is as unsatisfactory as a Committee that has no imagination and prepares a hackneyed and lifeless program.

In consulting with members of the club as to what subjects they would like to consider during the coming year, the Program Committee will probably be staggered by the great variety of suggestions and the absolute impossibility of handling such a miscellaneous assortment of programs in one season. When they go into executive session and leave indiscriminate enthusiasms and visionary ideals behind, they will ruthlessly strip away as much of the impractical wishful-thinking as they can and will concentrate on a few well-chosen programs which may not include everything of interest existing in this very interesting world, but will at least give the members a little useful information about a few subjects and awaken a response which will not evaporate completely as soon as the program is over.

Rule Number One for Program Committees should be: Do not try to cover too much ground in a single program, or in a single year. You cannot do justice to "Modern Art" at the October meeting, "Modern Literature" in November, and then polish off "Modern Music" in December. You couldn't come anywhere near doing a thorough job on any one of these subjects in one meeting. On the other hand, if you devoted a whole season of meetings to any one of these subjects, you would probably bore many of your members to resignation. If you tackle a big subject, concentrate on one important phase of it rather than attempting a smattering of the whole matter, which is all too often "a smattering of ignorance."

This is Rule Number Two: Try to select the essential phases of the subject. This will require some knowledge on the part of the Program Committee, and this leads us to Rule Number Three: Be wary of subjects you don't know anything at all about. Do not assign a member a topic far beyond the knowledge and experience of the individual members of the club, and do not import a speaker who is supposed to tell you all about the subject in three-quarters of an hour.

STUDY OF CURRENT EVENTS. Clubs that are studying current events cannot make a complete program for the year, but must build it as they go along. Very often it is possible for such a club to adapt itself to the constant changes which occur in world history during these times by outlining a year's programs containing only the fundamental subjects, and limiting the prepared section to only a portion, such as one-half or one-third of the full time, then using the remaining time for an un-programed presentation of the latest development. In this way, they can follow a fundamental outline of basic principles, and at the same time keep each meeting up to date. The prepared speech may be either preceded or followed by the "news commentator" and very often the two parts of the program link together in an unexpected way which heightens the significance of each.

For such a program as this, a monthly bulletin is advisable, to inform the membership as to what special features may be expected at the next meeting. This monthly bulletin is used by the informal luncheon and dinner clubs already mentioned, and also by other clubs which do not formulate a definite yearly program. The bulletin may be a printed or typed postal card, or a mimeographed sheet. Sometimes it is in the form of a sprightly personal letter from the Chairman of the Program Committee.

Speakers

This brings up the question as to just how far you should go in using "home talent" and to what extent you should rely on speakers from outside the club membership. Many of these latter are professional speakers and know no more about the subject you wish to hear about than you yourselves could find out by a little investigation at the public library and other available sources of information. Be sure that the speaker you are engaging is a real authority in his or her field.

PAID VERSUS UNPAID SPEAKERS. You may feel that your own membership is not capable of presenting programs of sufficient vitality to hold the interest of the other members, and that your club is too poor and obscure to secure good speakers, but you should not allow this condition to discourage you from making the effort to get speakers from the world outside, either for a very small fee or for no fee at all. If your group shows a real interest in current problems and is not afraid to go deeply into them from all sides, you will be surprised to find how many social workers, educators, state, county, and even national officials will be glad to come and discuss them with you for no fee other than, perhaps, the expenses involved in the trip.

In your desire to keep your programs alive and interesting, do not overlook the value of exhibits, demonstrations, maps, charts and other visual aids to presenting the subject. Many people are eye-minded and are much more impressed by what they see than by what they hear.

If you study current books and plays, remember that authors and critics like to keep in contact with their public, and often are as interested in talking to you as you are in listening to them, and their fees for club appearances are graded accordingly. If you include books in your schedule of subjects, you will find more response from your members if you take a contemporary author and in addition to studying one or two of his (or her) most significant works, try to get some first-hand information from him or his publisher about his life and his purpose in writing the books you select.

Some clubs build their entire year's program on addresses by

paid speakers and musicians, many of them people of national
and even international reputation. This is possible only for a
large club or a club with some prestige as well as financial resources in a large city. You may not be able to bring in paid
speakers for every meeting, but if you bring in only two or three
a year, you have some conditions which will govern your choices
and the success of your venture.

The Program Committee must know exactly what the budget
allows for this item, and should not exceed it. Some clubs invite
the public to hear their most distinguished speakers, and charge
an admission fee which is expected to carry all or most of the
expense. If this is done, it is wise to have the project under-
written (see Chapter X) and not commit the club to an indebtedness far beyond the budget in an outburst of optimistic
enthusiasm which may not be justified by events. Even with
underwriting, it is usually necessary to have an energetic committee busily engaged in selling tickets, for it is a strange discovery made by many clubs that the mere announcement of a
famous name and a date at the city auditorium does not of itself
guarantee a full house or a profit in the box office.

The question of just how far a club should go in asking
speakers and musicians to appear before it without fee is one
which has worried conscientious club officers more than a little.
This does not mean that it is impossible for you to get good
speakers and musicians without expense. It is only a warning
that you should not take too much for granted in asking for such
appearances and that you should do your best to see that the per-
former really gets what you promise him, a large and responsive
audience, favorable publicity, and, last but not least, gratitude
and appreciation.

It is always possible to get good speakers without fee who are
sent out by national organizations of various kinds, as well as
state and county departments. Some of these speakers, sent out

by commercial organizations, are frankly purveyors of "propaganda," but this need not frighten you if they make no secret of the character and purpose of the group which they represent.

Local musicians and speakers, writers and book reviewers often accept low fees from clubs in their home towns and are usually very generous in responding to last-minute calls, but no speaker or musician or other guest artist should be expected to appear for nothing just because he is a fellow townsman. On the contrary, the club should make a greater effort on behalf of the local "talent" than for the outsider.

In some large cities clubs pool their interests and conduct auditions at which Program Committee chairmen can hear speakers and musicians, meet them and talk with them before engaging them, but this is possible only in a few large centers. For the greater number of clubs, your Chairman and Committee must rely on the integrity of the agent of a lecture bureau, or first-hand knowledge and advice from some other clubs, or trust entirely on what they have heard about the proposed lecturer.

If you have engaged speakers or artists who are not club members, whether they are from your home community or from far away, there are one or two important things to be considered very carefully.

The Program Committee must watch its budget with the greatest care. Nothing is worse for the good name of a club, and also for its own morale, than to engage a speaker or artist and then not be able to pay the fee promised. Most contracts with speakers and musicians stipulate that payment must be made before the program and not after. This is merely a matter of self-protection and managers have learned over a long and painful period that this is the only safe way to protect themselves and their artists. Remember that while you may be taking a chance in engaging an unknown musician or speaker, he also is taking a chance to make a trip to your town to give you a portion of his life-work and vitality for what may seem to him to be a small reward.

MEETING THE OUT-OF-TOWN GUEST. Another thing is to send complete and detailed directions as to trains, both in and out of town, a notification of how the artist will be met and by whom. The visitor who arrives by train should if possible be met by a member of the Program Committee or an officer of the club and taken by private car or taxi-cab to the hotel or to the private house where he is to be a guest. If this is not done, at least the visitor should be informed in advance of the name of the best hotel in town and if possible a reservation should be made.

If your speaker or artist arrives just before the time at which he is scheduled to appear, it is more important than ever that he be met at the train, taken to the auditorium and to a dressing-room, not directly onto the stage. After a train or motor trip, no one wants to appear on a stage or lecture platform without a few minutes with a wash-basin, a comb and a mirror, and last but not least a few minutes of quiet in which to pull himself together and put his thoughts and feelings into the groove which they are to follow in his public program. It is to be hoped that your guest will not come directly from train or motor-car to the stage, and this should be avoided, if possible, when the arrangements are being made.

Another point which is absolutely necessary for the success of the program, both from your own point of view and that of the guest speaker, is that the business meeting preceding the program should not run over-time. It should be cut to the minimum and if for any unforeseen reason it runs beyond your schedule, someone (forewarned by an anxious President) may move that the business be temporarily suspended so that the club may hear the speaker of the day.

This applies not only to business meetings, but to other matters of purely local interest. Do not keep a speaker who has an international reputation as an authority on international relations sit, uncomfortable and bored, while a well-meaning but misguided club member reads a stodgy review of a current book, or a committee chairman reads a résumé of the latest governmental edicts on low-cost housing for coal-miners.

Next to keeping your speaker and your audience waiting long past the scheduled and reasonable hour, one of the worst offenses you can commit against good will and good taste is to keep the honor guest too long after the program. If you are planning a reception or any kind of a party at which he is to be (at least in theory) the center of attraction, the arrangement should be made long in advance of the date of his appearance. He should be asked if he wishes to attend such a reception,—do not take his attendance for granted. If you wish to honor him, do so graciously and not patronizingly. Many professional speakers and musicians who have to do a great deal of travelling, sometimes under rather uncomfortable circumstances, often find themselves so tired by a crowded schedule that any receptions, teas and dinners are just an added burden. No matter how great their good will and how appreciative of your offer of hospitality, they may feel that they must conserve every bit of energy in order to finish the tour and to give to their audiences their best efforts. On the other hand, do not feel that you should *never* offer hospitality to a visiting speaker or artist. Very often they are lonely and bored with travelling and welcome a friendly greeting, a dinner and over-night stay in a home and not in an impersonal hotel room, and a reception or a party after the program may be a bright spot in a rather trying existence. The point to remember is that such things should be a matter of courtesy and invitation and not just something to be taken for granted, at which the visitor is often the victim instead of the lion.

Participation of Members in Programs

Whatever the type of your club or the method of program you use, it is advisable to provide an occasional meeting in which some debatable topic is thrown open to discussion. The best way to conduct this is to ask three or four of your members who are good speakers to lead off with brief talks, not more than ten minutes each, and then allow remarks from other members in informal manner, not more than one at a time, however! The old-fashioned formal debate, with its rules and regulations, has its good points, although for club purposes an informal and unpremeditated discussion is usually better. Most clubs dealing with controversial topics allow a "question and answer" period after the formal speech. Even though this sometimes seems to be heckling the speaker, as a rule club members can be relied upon not to overstep the bounds of good taste, and speakers on public questions are usually quite used to questions, some of them frankly antagonistic. In many cases the speakers offer the question period to the club as an essential part of the speech, as this gives them a pretty definite idea of what public feeling is on that particular question in various parts of the country and just how their own ideas are being received.

The informal debate by club members tends to make the subject under discussion a live one to them, and not just an academic abstraction, and thus it tends to stimulate and sustain interest in the program. It also develops unexpected powers and abilities on the part of members, abilities which will be of great usefulness in the future.

Topics for club study and debate which were satisfactory twenty-five or thirty years ago are hopelessly out of date now and will drive members away from clubs rather than draw them in. The radio has been one of the most potent influences in this direction. News broadcasts have brought world events into every home, symphonic and operatic music is available to everyone, popular plays and books of the day are dramatized for the busy housewife, and club programs must compete with this new atmosphere in which we all live and breathe. It has been said that the American home has been deeply affected by the radio and the automobile, for the radio let the world in and the automobile let the family out. The same conditions apply to the club. Nobody is going to sit in a club meeting listening to a dull résumé of current events culled from the daily paper when they can turn on the radio at home or out in the family car and hear the latest events described and have their significance analyzed by people who really know what they are talking about.

Methods of Discussion

In addition to the presentation of papers and speeches, most clubs include in their programs a period of discussion, at which club members express their opinions in regard to the subject. These discussions may take any one of several forms.

One method is to have the speech followed by a question-and-answer period. Most speakers on important subjects are quite willing to submit to questions from the audience, and many of them invite such questions as it gives them a more accurate picture of the ideas and feelings of the public than can be gained in any other way. The presiding officer announces the question-and-answer period, after thanking the speaker. It is wise to announce the length of time during which questions will be answered, such as half-an-hour. Otherwise the questions may come in such numbers that audience and speaker will both be exhausted.

The best method of handling questions is to pass out slips of paper among the audience, on which questions may be written. These are collected by the ushers or pages and handed to the presiding officer. They may be handed directly to the speaker, but as a rule it is better to hand them to the presiding officer, who glances at them and hands them to the speaker for reply. In that way, obnoxious or ill-mannered questions (which are liable to turn up on any controversial question of great public interest) may be quietly eliminated without offending the speaker. There are also some questions which are quite irrelevant to the question under discussion and these also can be quietly eliminated by the presiding officer. Also the presiding officer, holding the questions, can watch the clock and at the proper time thank the speaker again and bring the meeting to a close. If the speaker has a handful of unanswered questions, he may feel that it would be ungracious of him to announce that he will not answer any more.

Subjects may be also discussed in the following ways:

DEBATE. The question to be debated is worded in such a way that it has only two sides, pro or contra, or yes or no. It may be a resolution, such as "Resolved, that women are more patient than men." One or two members are selected to advance the arguments for each side. A certain amount of time is allotted to each, and each side is allowed a "rebuttal," or second chance, when they may answer any arguments put up by the other side. At the end of a debate, it is usual to take a vote.

Debates are often used as a form of mental gymnastics, speakers advocating theories in which they themselves do not believe, just for the mental exercise involved in thinking up arguments. For this reason they are often regarded as amusing and entertaining rather than instructive. The subjects assigned (such as the one quoted about the relative patience of men and women) are of such a nature that they can be treated humorously. The debate is a kind of trial by combat, when two champions step

club, and it means that the subject and its treatment must be worth the attention of the public. When properly handled, a local radio period enhances the standing of the club in the community and also pleases the management of the radio station, as it indicates that they are living up to their responsibilities as an important and constructive factor in community life. A fifteen-minute period, once a week, will usually be sufficient and even that short time will sometimes tax the resources of the club. Radio offers a great opportunity to the service club which is able to measure up to its requirements, but the requirements of present-day radio are so strict that only an outstanding club with membership which includes many of the leaders of thought and action in the community can undertake to conduct a radio program.

The Club Year-Book

A fairly large and active club, with a wide range of subjects under study, will, if possible, publish a year-book giving the dates of the meetings for the coming year, the topics and the names of those taking part in the programs. This means that the Program Committee has started its work well in advance, has projected a carefully thought-out program, has arranged all details as to dates, speakers and other problems involved, and has done this work so well that it can announce confidently the club's program for a full year in advance. This is quite a task (though many clubs do it), and it indicates that your club is well-organized and functioning successfully. The year-book, which is attractively printed, contains also the complete lists of officers and committees and any other information about the club which may be valuable for members to have and interesting for outsiders to know. In printing year-books, always print a larger number of books than the exact membership of the club, as they can be used throughout the year for spreading information about the club throughout the community, and are always useful for reference.

If you are publishing a year-book, be sure to get estimates as to cost from several different printers and make sure that the printer you select is capable of turning out a good job. Samples of paper should be examined carefully, both for the inner pages and for the cover, and proof-reading should be done with great care, preferably by two or three members of the Program Committee. Do not leave the proof-reading to the printer, who is unfamiliar with your names and the subjects mentioned.

Do not forget to indicate on the front cover of the book the name of the club, the year, and the town in which it is located. This may seem an unnecessary piece of advice, but it is surprising how often clubs will issue pamphlets and books and neglect all mention of the town in which they are located, or the year for which they are printed, thereby causing great confusion and uncertainty to state officers, librarians, newspaper editors, and others into whose hands the book may come.

If you are going in for a year-book in a big way, you may publish the entire membership list, with addresses. Some clubs list only charter members, others publish an "In Memoriam" section listing those who have passed away.

Your year-book may be as elaborate as you please and can afford, or it may be the utmost in simplicity. A mimeographed sheet will serve to give the information desired, and for preservation it may be bound in heavy colored paper, tied with raffia or yarn, or a plain stout narrow ribbon, all of which can be done without cost to the club by the willing hands of loyal members.

Club Programs in General

Some clubs get along without any yearly outline, not because they cannot afford to publish a year-book, but because they think it inadvisable to plan so far in advance. Many of the successful luncheon and dinner clubs, of which we have already spoken, have carried on for years without planning their meetings more than a month or two in advance. This method works best in large cities, where celebrities and authorities on various subjects are easier to find than in smaller communities. An alert Program Committee for a representative group of business men and women, artists, writers and outstanding characters of the city can bring to the luncheons or dinners an almost endless series of interesting and worth-while speakers, some of them passing through the city and pausing briefly to visit the club, which they may have addressed several times before. In smaller towns and rural communities this type of speaker is not so easy to get on any certain date, and much the safer plan is to arrange well in advance for their presence and appearance before the club.

In planning a study program for a club, remember that group study of any subject is different in some ways from individual study. There is something to be derived from the contact of mind with mind which is lacking in solitary study. If possible, subjects should be presented in such a way as to stimulate thought, question, and discussion from the membership. If no time is allowed for discussion at the end of each program, a separate meeting may be set aside for a formal or informal debate on some of the questions posed by preceding programs.

XIV

How Papers Are Prepared

EVEN IF your club can afford to get all its speakers from outside the club membership, it is doubtful if this is the best method for building up a successful club.

To be sure, it *is* important to bring in to your club meetings men and women who are authorities in their various subjects. The benefits come not only from the facts and viewpoints which they bring to you, but also from the stimulus of new and striking personalities, a breath of outside air, a contact with the world of thoughts and events which may be quite foreign to your own existence. The presence of a speaker from outside should add to the variety of the discussion period following each lecture; and an occasional meeting may be given over to further discussion and debate.

Papers by Members

But more important than the contributions of outsiders to club life is the study and presentation of topics of vital interest by the club membership.

OLDER TYPE OF CLUB PAPER. Time was when "club paper" was almost synonymous with "dull." Members were assigned subjects and prepared their papers much as high-school students prepare "essays." Phases of history, the arts, geography, and similar subjects were handed out by the Program Committee, and the members went to the public library and to standard books of reference available to everyone and dutifully prepared a "paper" by copying and condensing the information found there. The literary style of the club papers was largely determined by that of the sources from which the material was obtained; there were plenty of dates and statistics, and though accurate the paper failed to fulfill its real purposes, for it failed to bring real information to the listeners because it was so dull and pedantic that the members did not listen intently. Also the paper failed to benefit the writer because it was a copy of some one else's thinking, a compilation of facts of no real significance. INFLUENCE OF RADIO ON STYLE OF CLUB PAPERS. That time has gone by. One of the things that brought an end to encyclopedic papers for club programs was the radio. Radio programs range all the way from hilarious entertainment to study of the most profound subjects, and these latter are presented in such a way as to entertain as well as instruct. The progress of medicine, science, invention, great turning points of history, great international crises are presented in the form of life-like and thrilling drama, or broken up into fascinating sketches. The total amount of time given to inspirational and educational programs is truly amazing and probably unrealized by the great majority of radio listeners, but it is so great that it has affected every phase of intellectual life.

Great as is the educational power of radio, and eager as are program-makers to avail themselves of it, they never forget that their greatest asset for getting and keeping the attention of their millions of listeners is entertainment. Like the theatre and the motion-picture, the radio aims to lift people out of the monotony of their daily lives and bring them release from strain and depression by amusement, entertainment, music, brightness, gayety, and above all,—drama. As unpromising a subject as diet has been discussed in a series of radio programs which has been one of the big successes on a national hook-up. How to get children to drink plenty of milk, and to eat spinach with enjoyment and not with complaints, these little sermons were not presented by dry talks of doctors and dieticians but by a series of short dramatic sketches, with brilliantly written scripts and skilful actors. The invention of vaccines, great discoveries in medicine, the discovery and development of vitamins,—all these and many other technical subjects have been brought to millions of listeners who probably never realized that they were being instructed, as well as entertained.

Of course, a club paper can hardly expect to be as thrilling as a radio drama, and the dramatic presentation is not recommended except when it can be accomplished with the skill that comes only from experience, but the underlying principle is still valid,—your paper must challenge the interest and attention of your listeners, it must entertain as well as instruct. Your audience is a challenge to you, and you must meet it with another and more compelling challenge in return.

EVERY MEMBER MUST PARTICIPATE. In a club which is well-balanced and which is carrying on its work like a sound and healthy organism, every member, sooner or later, should be called on to prepare and deliver a paper on a subject worthy of careful study in preparation and worthy of proper consideration by the listeners.

Whether the preparation of this paper is a privilege or a penalty when your turn comes depends largely upon your own mental attitude. If you are inspired by the desire to profit personally from the experience and to bring something worthwhile to your listeners, then you will undoubtedly turn out a paper which your fellow-members will enjoy and applaud. If you regard it as a disagreeable price which you must pay for the social opportunities and pleasures of club life, then your paper will probably be a failure. You will be irritated and depressed in preparing it and your audience will be bored and distressed when they listen to it.

Presumably we organize clubs to stimulate thought and to enrich our own lives by friendly contact and exchange of ideas. This cannot be accomplished merely by sitting back and listening, in a more or less critical spirit, to others. Your own development will depend on your own initiative and activity. You should welcome the opportunity to prepare a paper as an important step in the growth of your own personality. Merely reading extracts from magazine articles and the encyclopedia will not interest your listeners; and, worse still, it will not enrich your own experience or broaden your own horizon.

We have already considered the responsibilities of the Program Committee in choosing the subjects, selecting the speakers, and assigning the papers. Much of the success of the season's work depends upon the good judgment of the Program Committee in outlining the season so that it will follow some sort of plan, well-balanced with both unity and contrast. If their work is well done, the subjects on which members are asked to prepare papers are not vague and meaningless, covering too much territory, but rather the topics will be specific and pointed, involving individuals rather than epochs, particularizing rather than generalizing.

But, assuming that the Program Committee has discharged its duties to the best of its abilities, a successful season depends equally as much on the membership as on the Committee. Nothing can be more disheartening to a Program Committee which has wrestled for weeks with the devious problems of outlining an inspiring and enjoyable program for the season than to have the result of their labors greeted with an ensemble of protests, "Oh, I don't know a thing about that!" "I like Mrs. Parson's topic much better than mine; couldn't we trade?"

When Your Turn Comes

You have placed the responsibility upon the shoulders of the Committee; they have done their part; now it is up to you. Even if the subject you are asked to study seems not as attractive as some others, if you will make up your mind that you are going to do the best you can with it, you will probably be surprised at what interesting vistas open up before you after you have made the first step.

We have urged the Program Committee to begin its work months ahead of the actual program, if this is at all possible, and to announce the results of its planning at the earliest possible moment. We now must urge the members who are to take part in the program to begin their work also at the earliest possible moment. Even if the meeting at which you are to appear is months away, do not put off the preparation of your paper from week to week, for no paper worthy of your own and the club's time can be prepared hastily at the last moment. We all know about "Tomorrow and tomorrow and tomorrow" and "Procrastination is the thief of time," and all the other maxims and proverbs suitable to this subject, and we all know, alas, how true they are. You may be assured, in nothing are they more painfully even disastrously true than in preparation of a club paper.

How to Collect the Material

Rule Number One: Get started at once.

We have warned against the danger of depending too much on a hasty visit at the last minute to the public library or a frantic search in the encyclopedia. This does not mean that the encyclopedic, or public library approach is to be avoided. Quite the contrary. The library and the encyclopedia are your first sources of information, and should be turned to at once. The significance of the warning was not to allow yourself to depend entirely on these valuable sources of information, and not to copy and condense the information you find there and think you have studied the subject and presented it properly.

THE PUBLIC LIBRARY. Your public library should be your first source of help, but you must know how to use it efficiently. Librarians sometimes complain that the material which has been compiled so painstakingly and which they have catalogued and cross-indexed so meticulously is not used more often and more intelligently by the public. We have never yet heard a librarian complain that too many demands were being made on him or her, or on the material available.

When you go to the library, seek out the librarian and frankly ask for help. If you show an intelligent and eager interest in using the resources of the library for research, the chances are ten to one you will be greeted with an equally intelligent and eager response from the librarian who is flattered by your request for help and anxious to show how to use library facilities.

If yours is a large library with many departments, consult the head of the particular division under which your subject is classified. Don't expect the librarian in charge of fiction to give you advice about books on civic or financial problems. In most libraries, except the very largest, you will find a librarian who is fairly conversant with all the departments, and the co-operation of such a librarian is sometimes more valuable to you than that of a specialist, whose viewpoint may not be as broad, and who may not exercise as much imagination in tracking down material in unexpected places.

MAGAZINES AND NEWSPAPERS. Do not overlook the current periodicals and magazines, nor even the back-numbers of the standard magazines. In the periodical room the librarian will probably have "Poole's Index of Periodical Literature," or "Reader's Guide to Periodical Literature."

Your own miscellaneous reading in newspapers and magazines may bring you bits of information which may contribute to the value of the work you are doing. It is surprising how many things we hear or see in print about a subject in which we are especially interested. The items were probably there all the time, but until that subject became of unusual interest to us, we did not see them. Begin at once clipping out these miscellaneous bits and keep them in a large envelope. As the number of clippings grows, you may find it necessary to sub-divide and catalogue them. Recently a club member was asked to prepare a paper on the life of Stephen Foster, a name about which she knew nothing except that Foster was the composer of "Way Down Upon the Swanee River." The name caught her eye in a newspaper one day and she began a clipping collection on Stephen Foster. Within a few months she had over 300 clippings about a man whom she had barely heard of until he had been assigned to her as the subject of a club paper.

STATE LIBRARIES. If you live on a farm or in a small town which has no public library, do not neglect to make use of those libraries which you help to support with taxes—the State library, which is usually located in or near the State Capitol Building, and the library at your State University. Librarians at these institutions are usually glad to co-operate with you, because by proving their usefulness they can secure continued and larger appropriations for their work. They will help you to locate the books you are looking for, and will advise you as to the latest publications, and for the cost of postage or a small fee, you can borrow from them the books available.

A note to the Extension Division of your State University may bring just the help you want. Many such departments maintain travelling packet libraries, made up of clippings, bulletins, and reports on a great number of subjects. State Agricultural Colleges, Experimental Farms, Forestry Schools, Normal Schools, many of these public institutions have library service available to the public. Make yourself familiar with the resources of your own State government. You will probably be surprised at how much is being done along these lines, with your money and for your benefit.

In many states, the public library system is developed from state headquarters into county and town. Loans are made from county to town and school district, either by special arrangement or according to a regular schedule.

When you write to these out-of-town librarians, always state clearly the subject of your paper and if possible send a list of the books you have already consulted and others which you have heard about but have not yet been able to read. And do not hesitate to ask for information and advice as to further sources of information.

State aid goes farther than merely supplying books and pamphlets. Many states maintain Extension Divisions of Adult Education of State Universities and Agricultural Colleges which send out lecturers, slides and motion pictures for lectures and also suggest reading courses. It will pay you to write your state· universities and colleges for help and advice along all these lines.

FEDERAL PUBLICATIONS. Although many states have developed their information service to a high degree, probably the greatest source of information is the Federal Government. Few of us realize the wide range of information included in Federal publications, nor the extent to which it has been carried in many fields, ranging all the way from pamphlets to fairly large books.

So great is the amount of literature published by the Federal Government and so varied the range of subjects covered, it is impossible to give even an outline in such a chapter as this.

Over forty-five separate lists and catalogues are published and the list of these catalogues may be obtained by writing to the Superintendent of Documents, Government Printing Office, Washington, D.C. This list is issued free, but most of the publications themselves are obtainable for a small fee, ranging from 10 cents up.

If you know just what subject you want to study, write and ask for the price-list of publications on that subject, such as, for example, Public Health, Immigration, Adult Education, Forestry, Indians, Child Labor, and-so-forth. But if you are not fully determined as to the subject, the list of catalogues may be obtained, as described above, and a perusal of it will show you so many fascinating subjects for study that your trouble will be to narrow down your choice and not spread it out too widely.

If you cannot find your way around through the quantity of government publications available to you, remember that you can appeal to your Congressman for assistance.

OTHER SOURCES OF INFORMATION. And still you have not exhausted the available sources of material. Women's clubs may obtain much aid from the departments of women's magazines, which answer letters of inquiry along specific lines and send out leaflet and book material, usually at a small fee covering the cost of printing and postage.

Many large manufacturing concerns publish booklets regarding their industry which may be had for the asking. These booklets are not direct advertising for the product but rather histories of the industry and its development, and hence part of American history and economics.

Railways, steamship lines, travel bureaus, and State tourist agencies provide a wide range of valuable information in booklet form.

One of the important subjects now much under discussion is public health. For material on this subject, consult your town or county health officer, your City Board of Health, county nurse, head of your local visiting nurses' association, your local Red Cross Chapter, or perhaps most important of all, the Secretary of your State Board of Health. Almost all states now publish reports and bulletins about public health.

If your club is a member of a national organization or federation, you will of course make use of whatever material it may supply. The General Federation of Women's Clubs, 1734 N Street, N.W., Washington, D.C., has developed its departments to cover all phases of club work. The heads of the various departments either have printed matter which they will send you, or they know where to lay their hands on the material you want. (Also see Appendix for lists of organizations which will supply material for club study.)

How to Use the Material

You can readily understand why an early start was recommended. Unless your subject is an unusually obscure one, your problem will not be to collect a sufficient amount of information, but to analyze the large amount of material you will receive, select just what you want, and arrange it properly. The search for material, for most people who have any interest in the subject, is a fascinating occupation. You will at times feel like a detective following or discarding clues. From small beginnings your search leads on to unforeseen developments, one thing leads to another, and you will find plenty of use for your imagination and ingenuity, as well as perseverance.

Let us hope that the study of the material, when assembled, and the writing of the paper will prove equally fascinating. This will require considerable reading, and, what is harder, some good straight thinking.

If you have visited libraries, sent for some of the material we have suggested and consulted all available authorities, your desk is covered with books, reports, bulletins, and letters. Appalled at this mass of material, you exclaim, "How can I condense this into a twenty-minute paper?"

If you have started in time and are not pressed and disturbed by the near approach of the date when the paper is due, your task is not as hard as it may at first seem to be. The first task before you is one of selection.

Turn to the material which you have assembled: Here is a book which offers facts, dates, statistics. Here is a bulletin or pamphlet which describes some specific and perhaps highly technical subject. Here are newspapers and magazine clippings filled with anecdotes and human interest, something that you will need to accompany the facts and statistics if you are going to hold the interest of your audience.

Just to read the mass of material may be more of a task than you feel you can accomplish. Don't worry,—it will probably not be necessary. Do not try to absorb the entire contents of each book, report, pamphlet, and article. It can't be done. Learn to discard material that does not bear on your paper. Consult the table of contents before you undertake to read a whole book. You will probably find that several chapters have no connection with your paper. Do not spend time on them, at least for the present,—if you really like the book you can come back to those chapters after your paper is written and read them just for your own enjoyment. While you are at work, read only the chapters which will help you.

When two bulletins or reports duplicate statistics, select the one which bears the later date, or which deals directly with the phase of your subject you wish to emphasize. Learn to select only the most telling figures that will illustrate the major points of your argument. The repetition of mere figures, or too many figures, bores and mystifies the audience. Train yourself to select big, outstanding facts in all that you read, and make notes of them as you go along.

Getting It Down in Black and White

At just what point you first put pen to paper is a matter for you to decide. It varies greatly with individuals and is largely a question of temperament. Some students can hardly work at all unless they have first made an analysis of the subject and have written down an outline of the main points to be covered, a sort of table of contents for a book yet unwritten. Others cannot write a word until they have done most of the necessary reading and studying, and then have mulled it over in their minds and thought their way through the confusion into an orderly mental concept of the whole subject. This temperamental difference is to be found among successful writers and composers. Kipling is said to have written four complete and different versions of "Kim" before he was satisfied with it. Beethoven wrote and re-wrote and jotted down notes and memoranda until his note-books looked like battlefields, whereas Mozart had thought it out clearly in his own mind and when he began to write, the music flowed spontaneously along the lines he had laid out for it, and his first draft looked like the finished copy, without erasures, or changes.

You will quickly find out to which class you belong. Do not try to make yourself over. If you feel you must have an outline over which to train the vines of your thinking, by all means sit down at once and draw it up, and lean upon it heavily in the writing of the paper. If you are of the other type, don't let some kind-hearted friend tell you that you never will be able to produce a good paper unless you first make out an outline. No two people work exactly in the same way. Follow your own temperament and work along your own lines. The result will prove the rightness of your method.

The form and outline of your paper will depend to a great extent upon the subject-matter. Do not try too conscientiously to follow a set pattern which you may have read about or which you were taught in school. The introduction, the development, and the summation are a means to an end and not an end in themselves. The most important thing is the subject itself. If you have done some clear thinking as well as some intelligent reading, just try to present the subject as interestingly and as logically as you can, and the form of your literary composition will pretty largely take care of itself. Put yourself into the paper. Your own interpretation of the subject, especially if accompanied by real interest or even enthusiasm, will be far more appealing to your listeners than second-hand ideas copied out of a book.

If the subject is one about which opinions differ, do not be afraid to make up your own mind about it and express your own convictions, if any. Perhaps you may not be able to take a definite stand on some important controversial subject, in which case you will present the viewpoints and arguments of the opposing sides with fairness to all. But if you do have strong convictions they will infuse vitality and color into your presentation of the subject and will go a long way toward making a success of your paper, especially if a discussion follows your reading.

As you set to work on the actual writing, you may feel that you need a formula to help you. One of the best of these is: "What is it? Why is it? What of it?" Following this rule, you define your topic, then you present the background and history of it, and then you sum up the present situation, the probable or possible future developments, and your own feelings after careful study.

The subject may be one which requires considerable knowledge and use of technical language: Facts should be stated accurately, expert opinion quoted carefully, giving names and sources. If statistics and scientific facts are involved, be sure that they are up to date.

Your subject, however, may be one in which statistics and scientific facts play no part. Perhaps it is one which can best be treated humorously. This is one of the most difficult of all methods. Wit and humor are gifts of the gods. Do not attempt to be humorous unless you are sure of your ability.

Your subject and your personality may combine to make you feel that neither the methodical statistical method nor the fanciful and humorous are your best line. Perhaps the best approach is through a kind of middle ground, which we may call the colloquial. An easy, unpretentious way of saying things, perhaps even a rather intimate and personal method, will not lead you into either pomposity or frivolity. It gives you a chance to put your own personality into the manner of presentation, and will do more to win the interest and good will of your audience than any other method.

The shorter your sentences and the simpler your words, the more easily you can hold the attention of your audience. Write as you would talk to an intimate friend. Do not fret about literary style. Set down facts and opinions as simply, as directly and as sincerely as you can. That in itself is a successful literary style and your audience will respond to it.

Incidents, anecdotes, and personal experiences may help to hold the interest and illustrate your points if skillfully used, but do not weaken your paper by dragging in funny stories which have little or no bearing on the subject, just to raise a laugh.

After you have written the first draft, put it away for a few days and try not to think about it. Then when you take it out and re-read it, try to do so impersonally, as if it had been written by someone else. You may find that you have said the same thing twice or perhaps three times. Decide which is the best, and cut out the others.

You may find that the sequence of facts or opinions is not quite right. You may have said on page 6 something that should have been said on page 2. Try to make your thoughts move consecutively.

The use of certain words may not seem as correct to you on re-reading as when the sentences were first formed. A dictionary will give you some good advice on these questions, or better still a book of synonyms.

How Long Should Your Paper Be?

Finally, you may find that you have taken altogether too long to tell your story, to present your facts, and you will begin to cut out words here and there, to pull your sentences together, making them shorter, crisper, and more incisive.

If you are preparing your first club paper, by the time you have revised your first draft, you may feel like "trying it on the dog." A discriminating friend or a member of your family will serve as an audience of one. In this way you will find that some passages do not sound as well as they look in print, you will find points of weakness and also points of strength, climaxes which you may not have intended. Such a paragraph may be taken out of its place in the composition and put at the end, where a climax is more important and telling.

As to the length of the paper, the character of the subject and the amount of material involved will have something to do with this, and yet, no matter how involved or how difficult to condense, you must master the subject until you are able to compress it into proper length to hold the interest of your audience and to conform to the customs of the club. Unless you are an experienced reader, with exceptionally good diction, you must allow a minute for reading 100 words. Therefore, if the time allotted for your paper is twenty minutes, you must limit yourself to 2,000 words.

If it takes twenty minutes to read your paper, alone in your room, or before an audience of one, you should allow two or three more for slowing down the pace of your reading in the larger room, and the desire to make yourself understood, also for slight interruptions from the audience, such as laughter and applause, or unforeseen things like the arrival of late-comers. If your reading time, by yourself is 18 minutes, you can be pretty confident of taking 20 minutes for your public reading. Actors and announcers of radio programs have learned this valuable lesson and always make an allowance of about this proportion between the rehearsal time and the performance time.

Essentials of Presentation

Another unbreakable rule: Never apologize. Self-deprecation is always out of place in a public speaker. Don't apologize for your subject, for your manner of presentation, and above all don't apologize for lack of proper preparation.

Be sure that the copy you use at the club meeting is a good clear, clean copy, without erasures, omissions, or interlining. Be sure the pages are numbered and are in proper order. Copy books and note books are not advisable, as they look clumsy, and sometimes cause embarrassment if you turn the pages back to back, and then perhaps unconsciously reverse the process and find yourself scratching around for the next page. Loose sheets of paper, about book-page size if possible, are best. As each page is read, slip it under the last sheet in your hand. In this way the pages will stay in order.

The last bit of advice brings us back to the beginning: Begin in plenty of time to enable you to work unhurriedly. Do as thorough a job as you can in collecting and sifting material; write as simply and as convincingly as you can; revise with as impersonal an attitude as you can achieve, accepting or rejecting advice from friends and family according to your own judgment, (don't by any means accept *all* suggestions!); and then when you have done your best, stop worrying. Go before your audience as yourself, without pretensions or apologies. Your sincerity is the most valuable ingredient in what you have to offer, and your audience will recognize it and reward you with interest.

XV

How to Speak in Public

SOME PEOPLE have a talent for public speaking, just as others have a special aptitude for music, or mathematics. However, even where the talent exists, it must be cultivated and developed by study and practice, just as musical talent requires study and practice for its proper growth. It is true that a person without special talent for music should never contemplate a public career as a musician; but a person without special talent for public speaking may learn by observation, study, and practice both in private and in public and may develop an ability to speak in public which is quite satisfactory to both speaker and audience. Orators, it is said, are born and not made; but speakers can be made.

The First Attempt

Perhaps you *have* a talent for speaking which has been unsuspected, even by yourself, because it has never had a chance for expression. Many modest souls have been content to think of themselves as listeners until an unforeseen emergency got them on their feet in front of an audience, full of sincere and earnest conviction about some subject to which they have given more than a little thought and about which they really know something, and have suddenly discovered unsuspected

resources of ability to express themselves clearly and forcefully
and to carry their audiences with them. The years of listening
to all kinds of speakers, good, bad, and mediocre, have unconsciously taught them more than they realized about what is
good and what is less desirable in making a public speech, and
they have found almost by intuition the method best suited to
their own personality. If you are one of these listeners, do not
jump to the conclusion that you can suddenly rise to your feet
and become an accomplished speaker instantaneously. Please
observe that sincere and earnest conviction were mentioned
as prerequisites, as well as thought and knowledge of the
subject. And a long course in intelligent and discriminating
observation is also required.

Perhaps your education as a public speaker may not blossom
as quickly and successfully as this. Your first efforts may be
stumbling and faltering. Do not be discouraged. The funda-
mentals are simple and can be mastered by anyone who really
is determined to acquire the ability to speak convincingly in
public. They may not be acquired all at once and without some
sustained effort, but they are yours for the striving.

After you have taken the first plunge, experience will bring
you confidence as well as increased skill, but do not do all your
practicing in public. If you are inexperienced and doubtful of
your ability, there are a number of preliminary steps you can
take by yourself, and after you have made a few public appearances, no matter in how modest a way, you can grow by self-
criticism and by further practice and thought in your own home,
without any audience.

There are many forms of public speaking and each one of
them has some special technique or method differing from the
others. You may find that your forte lies in one or another form,
or you may be able to develop skill in more than one, for the
basic elements are much the same. You may read a prepared

paper, or you may deliver a prepared "set" speech; you may speak entirely from memory or from brief notes; you may be a brilliant impromptu speaker, or a skillful and persuasive debater, or you may be a witty and entertaining after-dinner speaker. It is not likely that you will excel in all, but you can learn to take part creditably in all.

Characteristics of a Good Speech

Let us suppose that you are inexperienced in public speaking and that your first assignment is reading a paper, such as we described in the last chapter.

When you are writing your paper, effective phrases and sentences will occur to you, phrases and sentences which will have force and power when spoken. Speak them aloud before you set them down—if you are in doubt as to the exact wording to convey your meaning, try out the possibilities by speaking them, rather than by writing them.

One thing to remember is that repetition is less noticeable in speaking than in writing. Great orators have not been forgetful of this, and some of the great orations of history, such as those of Cicero and Demosthenes, abound in repetition of ideas, though not always of exact words. Some of the most successful trial lawyers use repetition, subtly inserted in their words, as one of their best weapons. "I will prove to you," begins the Prosecuting Attorney, and after he has presented his evidence and arguments, he repeats, "I have shown you," "I have proved to you." This might seem like over-emphasis in print, but in the spoken word, it only serves to keep before the mind of the listener the whole outline of the subject and not just that phase of it under immediate discussion. Write your paper for the ear, rather than for the eye.

How and What to Practice

When you have written and revised the paper, and feel that it is practically in completed form, practice reading it aloud.

READING ALOUD. Try to speak naturally, without affectation, and yet with proper emphasis. Probably in the beginning you will find yourself either following a monotonous dead-level of tone, or over-accenting. Neither is correct and neither will hold the attention of your audience. No one can tell you exactly when you have hit the right accentuation for your own personality and for the subject of your paper. Do not try to be emotional over a subject which does not require emotion; do not be dry and matter-of-fact if your subject is one of warm human interest. These distinctions are not easily arrived at. Only by practice can you strike the right chord. There is no rule of thumb for manner and tempo. You must strike a happy combination of subject matter and your own personality.

When you have read your own paper over aloud several times, try reading something else aloud. Ten minutes a day of reading aloud with intelligence and growing awareness of good technique will do wonders. Read an editorial from the morning paper every morning for a week and you will find that you have gained in mastery of word groups and inflections, in pauses and in variety of tone. Try passages from the Bible, like the Twenty-third Psalm, or The Sermon on the Mount, or the speech of Saint Paul at Athens. Shakespeare is good practice. Try Portia's speech on the quality of mercy from "The Merchant of Venice"; Wolsey's "Farewell to Greatness" from "Henry VIII"; Marc Antony's tribute to Caesar in "Julius Caesar." It is not likely that you will want to use such a style in your club work, but the experience will give you a greater facility with words and phrases.

In your practice reading, try if possible to do it in a fairly large room, and use your full voice. Furtive *sotto voce* mumbling in a small room will not do you half as much good as using full voice, and imagining a fairly large audience.

You will probably feel slightly embarrassed at first and a little afraid of the sound of your own voice. This will quickly pass, and when it is gone you have passed the first milestone on your way to successful speaking. Your voice has now become your instrument, and you have begun to master it when you are no longer embarrassed at the sound of it.

Another good thing to add to your practicing at this stage is to speak in front of a mirror. Look yourself straight in the eye and it will help you later to look straight into the eyes of your audience. The first self-consciousness will soon pass away and you will be able to judge your facial expression and your bodily posture impersonally and when you can do that (and not until then), you will be able to control them and to improve them.

After you have read your paper or some other selected passage two or three times, practice raising your eyes from the page and looking out at your imaginary audience. Select the places where this can be done most easily, at pauses and at the end of paragraphs, then try looking up at less obvious places.

Keep in mind the value of pauses. Marks of punctuation like commas and semi-colons are almost invariably marked by slight pauses, and you will find other spots where a slight pause is effective and emphasizes the meaning. Here again you must be your own judge. Practice and observation will help, and intuition will guide you as experience adds to your skill.

A sympathetic friend or a member of your family upon whose interest you can count will doubtless give you a friendly reaction and offer suggestions as to manner of speaking as well as to the composition of the paper itself. But remember that no one else can get just the right shades and subtleties necessary to express your personality, which is yours and yours only. It must be *your* speech and expressed in *your* way, or it will fail to carry that sincerity which we have mentioned as the very basis of success. Do not hesitate to receive suggestions, and do not regard them as personal, but in the final judgment, follow your own intuition. If it is wrong the first time, there will be a second and a third time when you can correct your first mistakes. This is better than trying to do something which is unnatural to you and in which you do not whole-heartedly believe.

Try to keep your voice within its natural compass. Speak up loudly enough to be heard in the back row of your imaginary clubroom, but do not force your voice out of its natural range or quality. A mumbling speaker is no more irritating than a shouting one. If you force your voice too loudly, you will also affect its pitch, and the harder you force the higher it will go. Hold it down in pitch to its normal quality, but try to make it resonant and clear. You do not need vocal lessons to do this, if you have an attentive ear and an impersonal ability to criticize and evaluate your own efforts.

ENUNCIATION. Another point to watch is your enunciation. Many people have a slovenly way of talking, of which they are quite unaware. They run words together, they slur or completely omit some letters and syllables, they swallow many words half-uttered. When you listen to yourself reading, you may suddenly become aware of these faults in your own speech. The natural tendency is to "over-compensate" (as the psychologists say), and before you know it you are enunciating so carefully that your speech has lost all semblance of naturalness and spontaneity. Like the over-dramatic style, this is as objectionable as the fault which you were trying to correct. There is only one cure: Practice, practice, practice; and that means listen, listen, listen. You are training your ear as well as your voice, and you will notice the progress you have made the next time you listen to someone else make a speech. Slovenly? Affected? Gushing? Easy and natural, or stilted and false?

A method of improving enunciation highly recommended by teachers of elocution and expression is a drill in alliterative phrases such as you enjoyed in childhood:

"Peter Piper picked a peck of pickled peppers," you know how it goes. And "Round the rough and rugged rock the ragged rascal rudely ran," and "She sells sea shells, shall he sell sea shells?"

Too much attention to this kind of thing may make you self-conscious, but a little of it is beneficial, especially if practiced before a mirror.

GESTURES. Do not attempt gestures. They are almost invariably stilted and give an impression of affectation. As you gain in poise from repeated appearances in public, spontaneous move-ments of your hands or other simple gestures will come to you naturally, and they should be allowed to come freely and un-hampered, if they are a part of your own way of expressing yourself and not merely an effort to be more sophisticated than you really are.

Standing before the Audience

By the time you have read your paper aloud a number of times, you will find that it is half memorized and that you can read it slowly or rapidly, halting here or there, trying out different effects, and looking up from the page as often as you wish. This is the best way to go before your audience. A wholly memorized paper tends to become stiff and inexpressive, over-accented and often accented in the wrong places, for you have lost the real meaning of the sentences from too much repetition. An inexperienced speaker should *never* attempt to give a speech from memory. So much mental effort and concentration go into the mere act of memory that all vitality goes out of the message, and if the slightest untoward incident happens in the room, the thread of memory is apt to snap and then you are left in the humiliating position of the small child who has forgotten her "piece." Of all methods of public speech, speaking from memory is probably the worst.

When you step before your audience, do not rush headlong into your paper. Pause a minute and look at your audience as calmly as you can. Some teachers recommend counting "ten" before beginning. Better than this, trust your own judgment. This moment of calmness restores your nerves and tends to awaken your audience's interest. All public performers use it. Your preacher stands in his pulpit a few moments before he begins his sermon, the pianist sits quietly before the keys, sometimes for a full minute before touching them. Watch actors on the stage and in motion pictures and learn the value of pause, especially the initial pause. It has been said that "nothing in music is so effective as silence," and the same thing may be said with equal truth about public speaking.

SELF-CONFIDENCE. We will suppose now that you have made your first appearance as a public speaker by reading your prepared paper and that you have had an encouraging success with it, not a sensation nor yet a failure.

Do not ask for opinions about how well you did it, except from a few intimate and sympathetic friends. As for the public, just assume that it was well-done, and take it as much as a matter of course as you can. If you begin asking people how they liked it and telling them how nervous you were, and asking for suggestions, you will be putting ideas into their heads which otherwise would probably never be there. If they do not know it was your first appearance in public, they will probably assume that you are a veteran at it and will rank your performance much higher than you are likely to do yourself,—perhaps they will think you are better than you really were.

But from the helpful and discriminating few, do not hesitate to take advice. When you stepped out in public you became something to be talked about, like a gown or a hat, or a new automobile. Remember it is not *you* they are discussing and don't let your feelings be hurt by what might under other circumstances be a personal criticism. Public characters must get used to this, and from now on you are a public character, at least occasionally. Did you walk smoothly and naturally to your place on the platform? Did you stand correctly? Did your voice carry? Did you look up from the pages often enough? Did you make any awkward gestures?

Candid friends and family may make remarks that sting for a moment, but remember that they are talking about a performance, not a person. "Don't fidget with your handkerchief." "Don't fuss with that button on your dress." "Don't clear your throat so often." "Don't stare at the ceiling." "Don't laugh so nervously at your own jokes."

HANDS AND EYES. Two questions terrify the inexperienced speaker. They are "What shall I do with my hands?" and "What shall I do with my eyes?"

The best answer to these questions is "Nothing," but before you are ready to accept this dictum and act upon it, a few words of advice will help.

As to the hands, they should be left out of the picture as much as possible. One of the hardest things to do is to stand in front of an audience with your hands hanging motionless at your sides, until you raise one or both of them for a telling gesture. Practice this stance before a mirror. If it seems stiff and unnatural and if your nerves will not stand the strain of such complete relaxation, abandon it, at least for the beginning of your career as a public speaker, and ascertain by trial and error what is the most comfortable and natural position for your hands.

One of the easiest solutions of the hands problem is to hold a piece of paper in one hand. It may be a program of the day, or it may be notes of your speech. Do not clutch a button, or dangle a watch-chain, or play with your glasses. A promising career as a woman public speaker was seriously interfered with by a persistent attack of what a friendly observer called "bead trouble." There is also the story of the famous Prosecuting Attorney in a difficult case. His opponent had observed that when addressing the jury, this eminent orator always fondled the pendant of his watch-chain. When the day came for the final address to the jury, on which the whole case depended, the opposing attorney managed to remove the pendant just before the Prosecutor rose to deliver his masterpiece. His hitherto persuasive oratory limped and faltered, and he lost the case.

If your hands do not make you self-conscious in front of an audience, then forget about them,—they will take care of themselves. Usually only trained actors and orators can stand perfectly still with their hands motionless at their sides, and most of us have to hold something, but do this as unostentatiously as possible. Look over the platform where you are to stand and if there is a table or a stand or a piano or something else to touch, plan just what you will do, and when your time comes, do it naturally and forget about it.

As to the eyes,—here again the test is naturalness. Try to look directly into the eyes of your audience. You will find here and there a sympathetic face,—speak to that one. Another interested countenance will turn up somewhere else in the audience, and before you are through you will have collected a little group of real listeners. They are yours. Speak to them and forget the others. You will also find some blank, indifferent faces, some even antagonistic. If you have plenty of nerve, look directly at the unfriendly face for a moment or two now and then, and you may win a friendly listener. If they give you back an unrelenting glare, and your nerves begin to quiver, turn back to the friendly face you first encountered. All public performers are familiar with this strange and sometimes unaccountable division of their audiences into friends and enemies. A world-famous violinist recently said that if he found six or eight friendly souls in an audience, he was satisfied, and he played for them alone, forgetting the hundreds of stony countenances before him.

Do not try to include all your audience in your glance. Speak directly in front of you, with occasionally a side glance in one direction or the other. One sure way to lose attention is to turn constantly from side to side, endeavoring to take in the whole surface of your audience, like playing a garden hose on a lawn. You will end by losing them all.

If looking directly into the eyes of your audience intimidates you on your first public appearance, look just above their heads. This gives them the impression that you are looking at them, and relieves you of a sense of strain. Look just over the heads of those in the back-row and no unfriendly face will bother you. But this is just a beginner's device. As soon as your nerves steady down, try a few direct glances and the worst is over.

In avoiding direct glances, however, do not fix your eyes on some one object and keep them fixed with an almost hypnotic rigidity. You may glance at a clock, or a vase of flowers, or out the window, but only occasionally, never for long.

Stand still. Don't bounce around; don't drop your weight on one hip, then the other; don't teeter back and forth in a kind of orator's heel-and-toe dance. You will see experienced speakers committing these faults now and then, but they are definite faults and should be avoided. Don't take on any more bad habits than is absolutely necessary.

Developing Skill through Daily Conversation

After the reading of your first paper, you may feel discouraged and "let-down." You are sure you were a failure and you never want to speak in public again. You are like the aviator who has "cracked up," and the cure is just the same,—go up in the air again as soon as possible and this will help you to conquer your nerves.

Remember that your manner of speaking in public is a direct outgrowth of your daily conversation. A person who is slovenly and careless in everyday speech will not suddenly become silver-tongued when confronted by an audience. Most of us would be horrified if we had to listen to a phonograph record of our daily conversation, with all the hesitations and senseless repetitions, the unformed sentences, the fumbling for words, the use of meaningless clichés such as "I mean," "You know," "Really," "Well," and the appalling number of "ums" and "ers" and "ahs." Mispronunciation of words is not so common as misuse of them, nor is this fault found only among people of little or no education. The speech of a college professor may at times be full of unrelated subjunctive clauses, unfinished sentences,— pronouns without antecedents, subjects without predicates, verbs without nouns,—half-uttered literary allusions; if he had to listen to it on a phonograph record, he would not believe it.

In your daily conversation, cultivate the habit of expressing yourself in sentences, not in more or less related phrases. Don't say "really, you know, I mean, after all." When you have acquired the habit of expressing yourself clearly and accurately in your daily life, you will be able to do so in public speech, and not before. If you hesitate a little in choosing the right word, don't let that bother you. The right words will come to you spontaneously when you seek them. Sounds simple, doesn't it? It is simple, but foundation stones are usually simple.

At the next business meeting of the club, take part in the discussion, even if it is only a simple motion, or a second. When you have an opinion on a question under discussion, express it. Be brief and concise, but if you have a good deal to say and are convinced it is worth saying, go ahead and make a speech, not a long one, but long enough.

Progress in Public Speaking

You are now ready for the next step. You have taken part in club discussions and debates, you have prepared and read a paper. You are now ready to accept a topic for debate or for entertainment, and you are equipped by experience to gather your material, to arrange your ideas in logical sequence, to express yourself clearly and convincingly and to stand up in front of an audience and speak.

For this kind of speech the best technique is the use of brief notes. These may be written on cards which you hold in your hand, or they may be written on one sheet of paper which may be laid on a desk in front of you. Some very successful speakers and lecturers write down only the opening sentence and the closing sentence, with only a few key-words between, to keep their ideas in proper order. The opening sentence is carefully prepared in advance and delivered from memory (reminded by the note), and the closing sentence or paragraph is also carefully prepared in advance and repeated verbatim. The rest of the address or lecture is *extempore*. The speaker is so completely familiar with his subject, so sure of his facts and opinions, and so confident of his ability to express himself, that he stands before you and talks as he would if you were alone with him. This is the finest type of public speaker. It is not oratory, it has been called "exalted conversation." He is not hampered by trying to follow a memorized composition, nor to read a typed manuscript, nor does he flounder around in confusion of thought and hesitancy of speech. He has prepared his subject-matter, but not the exact wording. Successful lecturers may give the same lecture night after night throughout a whole season, always making it interesting and convincing, never twice the same. The audience reaction is a little different, the personnel of the audience is changed, the hall is larger or smaller, more imposing or more intimate, there are many things which may be slightly different, new words and expressions may come to him as he speaks, new phrases and new illustrations,—but the message is always the same.

When you have reached this point in your development as a public speaker, you may safely feel that you have arrived.

XVI

How to Get the Right Publicity

MANY A CLUB has had no real standing or influence in the community until a good publicity chairman exploited its activities in the local press. And many a club whose membership and attendance have been falling off, has been revived by the cleverness and resourcefulness of a newly elected press chairman.

Perhaps you think that your club does not want any publicity. Perhaps "publicity" to you means only the rather obnoxious appearance in the newspapers of certain names and faces, and those not always the ones you would most desire to represent your club.

Value of Good Publicity

But "publicity" means a great deal more than just getting somebody's "picture in the paper." The solid worth of proper publicity has only recently been realized and some of the former objectionable features are being eliminated. "Press agent" used to connote a tricky means of advertising theatrical and circus personalities. "Advertising" and "propaganda" carry unpleasant associations in many minds. The term "public relations" has been coined to denote a new conception of the relations of any organization with the public and to describe a new method of handling all forms of what used to be called "publicity."

Why not appoint a Chairman of Public Relations and give

serious consideration to the problem of presenting your club before the community in the best possible light, increasing its prestige and self-respect and avoiding any possible misunderstandings and prejudices?

For a small cultural club, whose main purpose is social and whose activities are confined to its own membership, publicity may seem unnecessary or even undesirable, but certain dignified items as to some of its more important meetings, its annual election of officers, and other such matters of public interest can certainly do no harm and will probably do some good. For any other kind of a club, proper publicity is absolutely essential. In fact, it has been said that for a club taking part in public and community affairs, proper publicity represents 50% of its working efficiency, and is worth all the officers, committees, resolutions and conferences all put together.

Consistent and well-directed publicity wins and holds community interest and builds up a fund of good will upon which the club can draw to assist it in accomplishing its objectives. It also builds up the club membership both in quantity and quality, as it attracts to the organization individuals who by themselves may be powerless to serve the causes in which they are interested, but who as club members become enthusiastic co-workers.

Proper publicity not only increases the vitality of the club itself, but aids enormously in the effectiveness of its work. Many worthy projects for community betterment owe their initial impetus and their growing strength in public consciousness to adroit publicity from some club which first realized their importance.

The Work of the Publicity Chairman

Such publicity must be dignified and informative and must be built up over a period of time by a consistent and constructive plan of action. It cannot achieve its purpose if it is spasmodic and haphazard. It must be planned and directed by someone who understands thoroughly what is being done and the methods by which it can be kept before the public. This means that your Chairman of Public Relations must be more than an enthusiastic and popular club member. She must be someone who is fairly familiar with newspaper and magazine conditions, and if no such person exists within your club membership, someone should be brought in from outside the membership or developed within the membership by experience and helpful co-operation from every branch of the club's life.

The Chairman of Public Relations should never be appointed carelessly, or to reward some deserving but poorly equipped member. Publicity is the most technical job in the whole club and the one who has charge of it holds a position of the greatest possible potentiality for either good or ill.

If you have in your club membership someone who has had actual experience in newspaper work, then you are indeed fortunate and there should be no half-way measures in co-operating with her for the good of the club. If you have no such person and must choose a member who is to take on this responsibility, try to find someone who has some or all of these qualifications:

1. She should be able to write well, and should like to write. No amount of personal ambition or devotion to the club will make a good Publicity Chairman out of a person who does not write well and who is known to be dilatory in answering letters, either personal or for the club.

2. She should have the capacity for making friends easily. This works both ways,—she must be on friendly terms with the newspaper people of the town and also must be friendly with the members of the organization itself, from whom she must be able to extract news items.

3. She must have or must develop by experience what is called "news sense," or "a nose for news." Members of the club will bring her items for publication which have absolutely no news value and she must learn how to separate the wheat from the chaff and how to do so without offending those whose "stories" are not published. On the other hand, editors and reporters will ask her for news and will soon become irritated and antagonistic if they receive from her only a miscellaneous collection of uninteresting details of routine club life. She must learn to recognize those events or business transactions at a meeting which will appeal to the reporter and editor and therefore secure space in the paper.

4. She must not play favorites in getting newspaper space for either people or projects. She must represent the entire club and all its activities, regardless of her own personal interests and preferences. She must handle with firmness as well as tact the importunities of those club members who love to see their names in print and she must be equally firm and tactful with those committee chairmen who think that their pet projects should receive the lion's share of club publicity.

5. She must show courtesy as well as efficiency to the representatives of the local press, and must secure and keep their co-operation. Every line of space given to a club is desirable advertising, as the clubs would soon find out if they had to pay for it by the inch. In most communities, editors do not have enough space to print all the news that reporters bring into the office and "write-ups" given to clubs are sometimes a favor and a courtesy. Recognize and acknowledge this courtesy and you will win co-operation from the paper and not grudging acquiescence. Too many club members think they are doing the editor a favor by sending in a "news item," consisting largely of a description of table decorations and dresses. More important is the news about the activities, the philanthropies, and the other

working plans of the club; if your club is a worth-while one, those are the things you want to be known for.

WHAT IS NEWS? While it is true that editors frequently print club news merely as a courtesy, it is equally true that the editor must make his paper interesting and an important factor in the life of the community, and he is as anxious to get hold of real news as you should be to have it printed. Many inexperienced Publicity Chairmen have sent out worthless stories of club meetings, concerned with trivial details, and have omitted to inform the editor of real events affecting the life of the community,—giving him something he does not want, and failing to give him something he does want.

There are many epigrammatic sayings about "news," but there is no one clear-cut definition as to just what it is. "A nose for news" may be to some extent an in-born talent, a gift, but it is more often a cultivated intuition, which is developed by experience, as well as by thought and observation.

Briefly, it may be said that the expected and commonplace is not news,—the unexpected or unusual is. This fact is expressed in the familiar adage, "If a dog bites a man, that is not news, but if a man bites a dog, that is news."

That, of course, is only partially true, but it contains enough truth and wisdom to be one of the guiding principles for the Chairman of Publicity. Very often an outstanding news-item *is* an important event which has been long expected and long delayed and when it does finally occur the newspapers rush to print it. Do not let the "dog bites man" theory blind your eyes to the importance of club happenings which are normal and usual, but still important.

Another newspaper adage which should be part of the working equipment of every good Publicity Chairman is "Names make news." Here again we cannot depend unquestioningly on the maxim as an infallible rule, but as a guiding principle it is of great value. Have you ever noticed how many stories in your daily paper are given out as interviews with some prominent person, or as announcements from some individual who holds a leading position in local or national life? For several years some of the most important bits of news from Washington were sent out as coming from "an unofficial spokesman for the Administration." Announcements about charity performances and benefits are usually attributed to some leading society woman who has given the use of her name as chairman of a committee, and who frequently knows nothing about what is going on. The president of a college or the president of a large corporation is quoted as having announced certain new developments or as expressing certain opinions, when as a matter of fact the developments and opinions are those of his subordinates. So it is in club life. Editors like to have a name to "hang the story on," especially if the name is one already pretty well known. Some project affecting the community life will be announced by the President of the club, or by the Chairman of the committee having it in charge, although it may be a plan on which many individuals have worked. The Secretary, the Treasurer, and the Auditor may work hard, but their work is not usually news, and they may never see their names in the paper. The Chairman of Child Welfare, or of Public Recreation or of some other work which affects the public directly may receive an amount of newspaper publicity which seems unfair to those other equally hard-working and devoted committee chairmen who are rarely mentioned, but that is something which cannot very well be avoided. The editor has to print news, and must be the final judge as to just what is news and what isn't.

But events within the club itself may be news if the Publicity Chairman knows how to handle them. A campaign for enlarged membership may be announced by the Chairman of the Membership Committee in such a way that it is of interest to the general public, and the name of the Chairman can be mentioned as the directing force back of the campaign. Benefits and performances to which the public is invited are always news. Routine meetings are not.

While we are on the subject of names, it should be said that one name which almost never should appear in the newspapers is that of the Publicity Chairman. She must be content to be the Power behind the Throne. The frequent appearance of her name as the source of club news arouses the jealousy and antagonism of other members, and it should be remembered that the public likes to think of the news in the paper as springing spontaneously from the original source and not being ladled out already cooked and seasoned by a "press agent."

Another reason for quoting names of officers and chairmen in news items is that good news stories are frequently expressions of opinions and viewpoints. A club may take sides in some local controversy and the editor of the newspaper naturally wants to express the policies of the paper on the editorial page and not in the news columns. If the club comes out in favor of keeping the public library open evenings until 10 o'clock, that should be attributed to the Chairman of the Library Committee, or to some other individual and not expressed in such a way as to line up the newspaper on either one side or the other. This fact is one reason why so much of our political news and especially accounts of the situation in international affairs are signed by the name of the writer. An anonymous news-story appears to be an expression of opinion or propaganda by the paper and all editors avoid this if possible.

THE USE OF PICTURES. Another phase of publicity which must not be ignored by the Public Relations Chairman, nor by the club members, is the question of pictures, either group or individual, and here again we must understand the editor's point of view. He uses pictures to brighten up his pages and to catch the eye of the casual reader. Naturally he wants these pictures to be attractive.

Group pictures are usually more interesting in local news than individual pictures. A small group of club members in the public park surrounding a tree which they have just planted, or perhaps a group of women seated around a table planning the details of a carnival for a worthy local project—things like this will often win a place in the newspaper.

CONTACT WITH EDITORS AND REPORTERS. In a woman's club, the cornerstone of a Publicity Chairman's success may be her ability to make friends with editors and reporters and to win their aid. Some papers prefer to write their own versions of club events, and they should be allowed to do so if they wish.

Another important aspect of the relationship between club and press is the treatment of reporters at club meetings and conventions. An efficient Press Chairman will see that the press representatives are provided with good seats, and a proper place to write as well as to see and hear. If possible, copies of important speeches will be handed to them in advance. If the meeting is accompanied by a luncheon or dinner, the reporters should be seated at a table together or at tables with club members. Everything should be done to make them feel that they are welcome and that their efforts to report the proceedings accurately and attractively are appreciated. (This is especially true at conventions, which we will discuss in a later chapter.)

How to Prepare Copy

In preparing news items for newspapers, your chances of success are greatly enhanced if you will follow a few simple rules.

Copy should be typed if possible, and in this day and age it is almost always possible. Double-space your lines and leave a wide margin.

Write on one side of the paper only. This is absolutely necessary. In most newspaper offices, a news item in long-hand, on both sides of the paper, would be considered nothing less than a crime.

In telling your story, get the most important fact in the first sentence, somewhat like a headline in the newspaper. "A campaign to have a neglected west-side lot turned into a city playground was begun yesterday by the Contemporary Club, according to a statement issued by its President, Mrs. Norman Peale." That's your story and what follows the opening sentence is the tail to the kite.

Omit as many verbal bouquets and expressions of opinion as possible. Use simple words and short sentences. Be accurate, be specific, be brief. A well-known newspaper in one of our largest cities has a framed motto hung in a prominent place in the reporters' room: "The story of the Creation of the World was told in 823 words."

News writers have a formula which they call "the six honest serving men,"—the words, Who, What, When, Where, Why, and How. When these six monosyllables have served you, your story is told.

The Publicity Chairman must know the "deadline" of all the newspapers which may publish club news. The daily papers have a deadline after which no news items will be accepted for that day and by the following day they are not considered news, so "dead line" really means "dead" as far as your news is concerned.

Most daily papers publish special departments on Saturday evening or Sunday morning, and for these the deadline is usually Thursday. Have your copy in by Wednesday if you want to get a good location on the page. Newspapers in small towns and rural districts have their deadlines too which should be scrupulously observed, even though their schedule does not seem as compelling as the more rapid-moving city daily.

Very often the editor will accept a brief statement as to a club event such as election of officers, award of prizes after a competition, or a banquet or club play, which is published in the paper on the day following its occurrence, and then he will (sometimes) also accept a more extended account for his special page of club news on Saturday or Sunday. This can only be done if the second and fuller story contains elements of interest to the public, as well as to club members, but you are co-operating with the editor in his plan to keep his daily news columns brief and up to the minute, reserving the more personal and comprehensive review of special events for his weekly edition.

Where two or more papers are included in the scope of your publicity, be absolutely fair with them and send your news items without partiality. If one of the papers sends a representative to you for further news and is anxious to publish more about your club, that is a matter for the editors to decide among themselves, but on your part be sure that you are not saving your best news items for one paper and ignoring the others.

Co-operation of Officers and Members in Handling Publicity

Successful publicity about club events requires more than a hard-working Publicity Chairman, no matter how capable. It requires the complete co-operation of every department of the club and of every official from the President down.

If she has no typewriter of her own, then the club should buy or rent one for her. She should have an adequate budget for stationery, postage, telegraph and telephone.

She should have news from every officer and from the chairman of every committee. She should never have to beg for it, nor wait for it.

She should have a correct list of names and addresses of all club members, so that she can verify the accuracy of names and addresses in sending out news stories, and also so that she can make her own inquiries if necessary as to just what took place and where and when. This list should itemize the various committees and their chairmen.

Last, but by no means least, she should have full charge of all publicity sent out by the club or concerning the club. It is absolutely impossible for any Chairman of Public Relations to build up a consistent and constructive publicity campaign for the club if she cannot control the situation, both as to quantity and quality of material sent to the papers.

Chairmen of other committees should be especially careful not to issue their news stories without consulting the Press Chairman. Sometimes an enthusiastic chairman will be so full of jubilation at the accomplishment of some project that she will be impelled to call up the local newspaper, but she will find that her news should be released in relation to the rest of the club publicity, and this can only be determined by the Press Chairman.

This does not mean that the President and Committee Chairmen can never say a word to reporters or allow themselves to be interviewed. It only means that such things should be done with the knowledge of the Press Chairman and in relation to the whole scope of club publicity.

XVII

The Community Service Club

CLUBS may be divided into two groups: those that serve their members only; and, those that serve the community.

The first group includes all clubs whose programs, lectures, and social privileges are offered to members and invited guests only.

The second group includes those clubs whose members combine with a study program some allied projects which help the community. The club members follow the study course, but the entire community shares in, or profits by, its activities. Many clubs have started out as cultural clubs, with programs for the pleasure and enlightenment of members only, and then have felt the urge to put some of their study into practice and have from that time on taken an active part in community life. The club which goes in for practical service does not need to give up its cultural and social aspects. It merely enlarges its scope, and frequently finds that the programs of study have been greatly enhanced in interest and importance by the addition of the practical to the theoretical and analytical.

Choosing the Club Activities

The selection of the means by which your club will serve the community and the nation is something which must grow out of the character of the club. Some clubs are organized for specific forms of activity, others for cultural and social activities, out of which practical work will grow. Only the largest clubs can operate along a number of different lines, with well-organized departments. Most clubs are well-advised to stick to two or three subjects and do a good job on these rather than to attempt to cover too much ground and spread themselves out so thin that nothing of any importance is accomplished. However, in a club of varied interests, it is quite proper to select one or two subjects, concentrate on them for a year, and then turn for the program of the next year to something else.

In selecting or planning activities for the club year, officers and chairmen should consider the interests and tastes of the membership as a whole, rather than the wishes of a small but enthusiastic group, or even community needs. In carrying out any activity, the co-operation of the majority is needed.

When plans for community service are being laid for a club of fifty members or less, the chairman of the committee may send out a typed or mimeographed questionnaire listing the needs of the community or the suggestions already offered. Members are asked to check the activities in which they are most interested and return the questionnaire promptly. The activity securing the most votes will then be chosen for the club's major activity during the coming year, unless the officers of the club feel that the question needs further discussion at a meeting of the full membership.

After the activity or activities of the coming season have been chosen and agreed to by the club membership, probably the best method of procedure is to elect or appoint a Committee on Co-operation. If the club is not large enough to warrant a special committee, the Program Committee can be given the responsibility of inaugurating and carrying on the work, but if the club is large enough, it will be found useful in more than one way to have a Committee on Co-operation.

The first duty of the Committee on Co-operation is obviously to keep in close touch with the Program Committee in planning the study programs for the year. When this is done, the Committee on Co-operation is responsible for all conferences with town and county authorities, including the Chamber of Commerce, the Grange, the School Board, or any other organization or public official with whom the club will come in contact in carrying out its plans. The hearty co-operation of outside agencies is absolutely necessary to the success of the club's efforts. Indifference or downright antagonism may be encountered at first, but this can be overcome by tact and persistence until all concerned are convinced that the club means business and can be counted upon to accomplish what it sets out to do.

Another important function for the Committee on Co-operation is to secure accurate and complete information about the conditions under which the work is to be accomplished. Unintelligent and uninformed outbursts of enthusiasm will not be welcomed by public officials or organizations. The club must have facts upon which to build its work.

The Chief Club Projects

Complete statistics are not available as to just what work has been accomplished by clubs during the past decades, but all the information which has been gathered, (and it is of sufficient amount to be regarded as giving a fairly accurate picture of the total), indicates that three subjects have led in interest and the amount of work accomplished. They are (1) Libraries, (2) Community improvement, and (3) Student loan-funds.

LIBRARIES. The subject which has interested the largest number of clubs and has been most benefitted by club activity and co-operation is the public library. Reliable figures on social service prove beyond question that more than 80% of the public libraries in the United States owe their existence to women's clubs, whose members raised money to buy the first books circulated in the community, or who paid rent on the building or room in which the first library was housed, or who created the public sentiment which resulted in establishing a library.

Your town may be well-provided with a public library, but there may be plenty of work to do in enlarging its scope, in bringing its material up to date, in beautifying the building, and in building up greater public interest in it and greater use of it. A field which is comparatively new and in which there is almost always work to be done is in bringing the library within the range of grade-school education and bringing the children to the library. A special room or department for young people, special hours for their benefit, story-telling hours for the younger ones, pictures and exhibits for the older ones, trained or volunteer helpers to assist with "home work," special music hours, art exhibits (prints of great paintings),—all these and many more activities are needed and can best be accomplished by public-minded club members.

Another field for active and worth-while club work is the growth of the rural library, whereby books are taken to the farmers and their families, rather than expecting the country folk to come into town for their books, even if the books are available for non-residents. This rural library movement is growing all over the country, but it needs help. Public interest must be aroused, more and specially selected books must be available, and book-trucks must be provided, with drivers, to distribute and collect the books.

Do not think that there is no further need for your help in the public library systems of the country. In spite of all the progress that has been made, there are still approximately forty-five million people in these United States, about one-third of our entire population, who are without access to public libraries.

COMMUNITY IMPROVEMENT. First in point of popularity with clubs (according to the number interested and the amount of work done) is the Community House. This has been especially successful in small towns surrounded by rural districts. Many such towns received a new impetus of civic pride when a local club rented and furnished a rest-room for the wives and children of farmers who trade with local merchants. The practical value of the rest-room having been proved, the community became ready and eager to raise the needed funds for a Community House, which became the center of many local activities never dreamed of by the courageous club women who first rented a storeroom on a downtown street, did the cleaning and decorating with their own hands, and volunteered so many hours a week as individual hostesses.

Another club activity which has left its impress on a large number of towns is a combination clean-up and beautification program. The amount of work which has been accomplished along these lines by the initiative and persistence of club members (who had a lot of fun doing it) is incalculable. "The rake, the hoe, and the bonfire" was adopted as a slogan by many clubs, and "Put the jinx on junk" was the motto of one particularly energetic club. Clean-up drives literally swept the country a few years ago, practically all of them started and carried on by clubs. Vacant lots were turned into gardens, playgrounds fenced and provided with equipment, unsightly billboards were removed, tables, benches and out-door fireplaces were provided for public picnic-grounds, smoke nuisances were abated, the town street-cleaning department was awakened from its long slumber, a thousand and one details of beautification were attended to. At first the effect seemed small but the greatest achievement was always the awakening and intensification of community consciousness and pride.

Closely allied to the improvement of the externals of community life is the subject of public health, and here again the club has been able to accomplish much more than the individual private citizen or even the elected officials could do. A brief list of projects successfully carried through by clubs will give only an inkling of what has been and can be accomplished. Towns have benefitted by the installation of maternity centers; baby clinics; health examinations for pre-school-age children; child guidance clinics; day nurseries; dental clinics; public swimming pools; drinking fountains in public squares and parks; proper milk inspection; study and care of underprivileged children, including summer camps; visiting nurses. STUDENT LOAN-FUNDS. The student loan-fund has been one of the most popular and successful activities for clubs. Over two million dollars is now in use in scholarship funds. As fast as it is repaid by students who have benefitted by it, it is loaned out again to some other worthy and ambitious young person. Most of this large amount is held in small sums by individual clubs and is loaned out in even smaller sums. Much of the money has been raised by simple means, benefit performances of different kinds, cake sales, and other local activities of individual club members. All kinds of students have been benefitted—for high school and college, for special training in the arts and professions. Some clubs handle their own funds, others allocate certain amounts to near-by colleges and schools, to be awarded by them according to their own judgment. There is no other "security" than the character of the applicant, and the percentage of loss is almost infinitesimal.

AMERICAN CITIZENSHIP. In communities with a large number of foreign-born, work in the field of citizenship is called "Americanization," but there is work to be done among native-born citizens, and a more comprehensive title for the study and work by clubs is "American Citizenship." Study of our form of government, its origins and variations during the course of history, often leads directly into more active participation in public affairs. It is not necessary for any club to align itself with any one political party in order to study and act on local, state and national problems. Study the administration of law and justice in your own community in order to understand how to correct any abuses which may exist; arouse interest in public affairs by conducting informal "Citizenship Institutes" where citizenship is discussed; find out how citizenship is taught in your own public schools and try to improve its methods if they seem to need improvement. These are only a few of the activities you can carry on among American-born citizens, and when you begin to study the problems connected with the Americanization of foreign-born citizens, your opportunities increase. This work requires a fine sense of humanity, breadth of mind, and a great love of people, as well as enthusiasm, and knowledge of the subject.

EDUCATION. We have already spoken of student loan-funds as a club activity. There are other aspects of education in which clubs can and do play an important part. Among these are: night classes for employed and especially for foreign-born; part-time classes and continuation schools for those who wish to supplement their limited educations; classes for adults in home economics and in various trades. You can work to develop the kindergarten system in your local schools; help to secure motion picture equipment and good educational films; put on a campaign to equip your schools with musical facilities, pianos, radios and phonographs with records; help to establish or to develop the high school band, encourage it by helping to purchase new instruments and also by attendance at public performances; help to provide good picture and educational exhibits for school use, and co-operate with the school authorities in every possible way to make the school attractive both inside and outside.

INTERNATIONAL RELATIONS. One of the most important subjects for club study is International Relations. It may seem to you that this is a realm where there is nothing you can *do,* but even if your activities go no further than intelligent study of the complex problems of the modern world, you are doing something. If you can engage an authority on public events, a professor of political economy or history from the State University and make this lecture free to the public, followed by a question and answer period, you have done something. You can also co-operate with local organizations in arranging public-meetings at which an outlet is provided for local opinion on the questions of the day, and you can, perhaps, co-operate with local clergymen in putting on special services, featuring such topics as may properly be discussed under such auspices.

The Arts

The so-called "culture clubs" have specialized in the study and enjoyment of the fine arts, but many of them have been led by their study into a desire to play some practical part in the life of the community, and have become "service clubs," while still maintaining their study programs.

There are many ways in which clubs which have studied the arts and have acquired standards of taste and judgment can increase both the quantity and quality of artistic awareness and appreciation in the community.

MUSIC. One of the first plans which will occur to you in regard to music is to put on a series of concerts at popular prices. This is one of the most important contributions your club can make to the community. In order to meet the expense involved, a guarantee fund must be raised or subscribed in advance, and it is also wise to have a group or several groups of ticket-sellers who make a consistent campaign before the opening date. It is usually advisable to put your emphasis on selling tickets for the whole course rather than for only one concert.

But there are other musical activities which can attract the interest and energy of club members. Music in the public school is sometimes far behind other cultural subjects and a little enthusiastic co-operation from parents will sometimes put new life into the music courses. High school bands are a commonplace nowadays, though they were an exciting novelty only a few years ago, but they can still be helped to greater usefulness. How about the books on music and the biographies of great musicians in your public library? Community sings are popular in many districts, especially the singing of carols at Christmas time. Other public institutions beside schools and libraries may need and would appreciate phonographs with records, and also radios. National Music Week (see address in Appendix, page 292) has many suggestions for fostering music in your community.

LITERATURE. Perhaps literature as a whole is more widely appreciated than music. It is more accessible and more easily understood. We have already mentioned the co-operation with public libraries as a leading club activity. Another aspect of literature is the stage. Plays and historical pageants frequently catch and hold community interest.

PAINTING AND OTHER ARTS. What we call "Art" does not mean only the paintings of great masters, which may be inaccessible to you, except in reproduction. Along with your study programs of the lives and works of Rembrandt, Raphael and other great men, do not overlook the humbler industrial arts. Even in small communities, exhibits can be made of objects collected from homes.

Fine work in textiles, embroideries, pottery, baskets, and rugs should be emphasized, and in this field we will sometimes find that our foreign-born neighbors may have much to teach us.

When you are studying any of the arts, the American artist should always be kept in mind. There has been in years past a prejudice against the American musician, painter, poet, and a prejudice in favor of the foreign-born artist. There was an exotic charm about the foreigner which our own neighbors seemed to lack. But this day is rapidly passing away. American literature, painting, and music have passed beyond the stage of immaturity at which they could be "encouraged" in a condescending way. The arts have matured in America, and it only remains for us to make a wider place for them in our daily lives and to enlarge their public and deepen their influence.

OTHER CLUB PROJECTS. There are many other subjects which have been found profitable for study and action by many clubs, such as proper marking and preservation of historical places in the locality, or participation in campaigns for safe roads, or matters of public interest concerned in local, state and federal legislation.

XVIII

New Clubs For Old

PERHAPS you belong to a club which has been jogging along for so many years that it seems to be going on more from habit than from any vital moving force. The same old programs, most of them no longer stimulating, the same old group at the meetings, slowly dwindling as the years go by, few new members and these making no contribution to club vitality, a general sense of complacent lethargy,—all these symptoms are apparent to you and make you feel you want to do something.

There are three courses open to you: (1) You can resign and join another organization; (2) you can undertake a campaign to reorganize and revitalize the club; or (3) you can resign and form a new club.

Changing from One Existing Club to Another

The first solution is the easiest. If there is in existence in your community a club in which you feel you would be more at home and through which you think you could broaden your own experience and also be of some service to your community and nation, probably the best thing to do is to resign from the old organization and apply for membership in the livelier and more dynamic group.

Giving New Vitality to an Old Club

But possibly you have a feeling of affection and loyalty to the old club and you may feel that its long tradition of service and helpfulness deserves a better fate than slow death. There may not be any other organization available to you which fits the requirements of what you feel your club ought to be. You do not want to desert the old club, you would miss many pleasant associations; you do not want to be accused of disloyalty; you would like to put new life into it and be a part of its revival. Then you will choose the second solution, and this is the most difficult of the three.

You will have need for all your tact and diplomacy, for all the qualities of leadership which you possess, and above all for patience and good will. You will meet with antagonism, some of it good-natured, and some not so good-natured. Whatever you do, do not think that you can reorganize the club single-handed or that you can force your own ideas and plans on the officers and membership against their will. The only possibility for success is through enlisting the co-operation and devotion of a small or large group, who in turn will bring influence to bear on the others.

If you think the club is worth saving, sound out a few of the other members in informal conversations, trying to analyze the trouble and bring out suggestions for remedying it. Do not attempt a sudden overthrow of all the old officers, many of whom have spent years in one position or another. A gradual building up of new activity on the old foundations will in the long run bring about the rejuvenation you desire, whereas a drastic move would arouse more antagonism than support among those members who have not given much thought to the problems involved. It is not only that you wish to avoid hurting people's feelings and do not want to turn friends into enemies—that in itself is bad enough—but above all you do not wish to defeat your own purposes by throwing the club into dissension instead of bringing into it new energy and purposefulness.

Perhaps the adoption of a policy of active service in the community will bring about the desired new vitality. "Stop talking, and go to work," has been the salvation of many moribund clubs. Your problem may be no more complicated than to introduce a new study program accompanied by an active campaign for some form of civic betterment.

Your first thought will probably be the inclusion of new members. A campaign for new membership can be organized, putting to work on it those members of the club who feel as you do about the need for new blood.

But new members almost certainly will require new program activities. With dull and hackneyed programs leading nowhere, new members are not likely to be attracted to the club, and without new members you may have difficulty in revising the programs. The two problems go together, and the solution of one will help to solve the other. You must work out a plan in which each phase of the combined problems will react favorably on the other. More stimulating programs will interest the new members, and once you have got the new members inside the organization, put them to work. Do not let them feel for a moment that they are outsiders and that they must be content to sit quietly and listen to the older members. This is especially important if your project includes inaugurating a new project of practical service to the community.

It may seem strange to suggest raising the dues as a method of putting new life into an old club, but this prescription has worked wonders in more than one instance. If increased dues mean increased activity and interest, the move is often stimulating to a high degree, although it may be hard to persuade some old members that the established custom of years has to be done away with. In some instances, the dues are too high for the activity of the club, and in that case they may be lowered with beneficial effect, but in the majority of cases, the exact opposite is true.

Another prescription for reviving moribund clubs is to affiliate with some national body. If your club has never focussed its attention on any practical activity for a long enough time to make its influence felt and to maintain the interest of its members, perhaps a new impetus may come from the contacts which can be established with a national organization moving in the direction which your club has followed waveringly. (See list in Appendix.)

Perhaps if the work of your club is departmentalized, a new strength will come into it from greater concentration of effort. Instead of a rather sprawling program in which everybody is only mildly interested, a few small and lively committees may bring in new intensity, new purpose, and the whole club will benefit.

Organizing a New Club

But if you have canvassed the situation in your own mind and in conversation with a few club friends and have decided that the old club is past redemption, or that it is not the kind of club you are ever going to be interested in, and if there is no club available into which you want to put your time and efforts, then the third solution,—to organize a new club,—requires your consideration.

There are doubtless many good reasons for organizing a new club, but remember that there are thousands of clubs in existence already, many of them working together in strong national federations. Duplication of effort is a waste of time and energy.

Don't organize a club just for the fun of it. There is plenty of fun in it, but the pleasure you will derive from it should be a secondary and not a primary reason for bringing it into being.

Don't organize a club if a similar one is already in existence in your locality and doing good work. Don't organize a club merely because you think somebody else is getting too much publicity out of club work. Don't organize a club for working purposes unless you are reasonably sure that you can gather together a group which will really accomplish something.

Try to make clear in your own mind just what you want to do, and give careful thought to the selection of the group you wish to invite to organize with you. Unless you select your organizing group with care, you may find your project defeated or at least diverted from the aims you had in mind.

Study carefully the list of national organizations given in the Appendix. Make a survey of existing organizations in your own community. Even if there is no club of exactly the type you are thinking of, there may be one of similar character which perhaps is not accomplishing the purpose for which it was created. Perhaps that group needs your help. The organization of a similar club, even though not exactly the same, might be interpreted as opposition or rivalry and do more harm than good. On the other hand, your investigations may suggest to you a need for a club of somewhat different type than the one you had originally planned. Your survey will give you a deeper insight into the whole question of organization and you will doubtless be surprised at the number and variety of clubs already existing.

This is especially true of women's organizations. There are so many good reasons for them, partly because of the radical changes which have come into the lives of women during the past fifty years or more. The original idea of culture and mutual helpfulness which brought the first clubs into being still holds good, and this in itself may be a valid reason for organizing a club in communities where it does not exist. But there are many other reasons. The homemaker has found that social and political problems as well as problems of public health and welfare affect her home. She cannot take a passive role in the solution of these problems, and is not content to have them worked out for her by others. She wants to have a hand in anything which affects the welfare of her husband and children as well as in the things which affect her alone. As an individual, she is handicapped and ineffective. As a member of an organized group she becomes more closely identified with the life of the community and becomes part of a force which cannot be ignored in any aspect of communal life.

While the idea of organizing a club is germinating in your mind, talk it over informally with a few of your friends and acquaintances. If you feel that a club could make a real contribution to civic or rural betterment, do not hesitate to call on some leader in public affairs and sound him or her out as to what might be done. These conversations are a necessary part of the survey you are making of existing organized groups, whether they are called "clubs" or not. Town, county and state officials may give you valuable and unexpected information as to conditions.

THE FIRST INFORMAL MEETING. When you have collected your information and have made up your mind, the next step is to make a list of people who may be interested in the sort of club you are organizing. Invite these individuals to your home or some other appropriate place to discuss the project. The group should be a small one, perhaps not more than four or five, and the invitation may be a personal one from you, or it may be a written invitation signed by two or three of those who are interested in the idea. You may use your own judgment as to whether or not you will include in the invitation an outline of what you propose to do. In most cases, it would probably be wise to do so. State clearly the type of club you are forming, so that they will come to the meeting with some feeling of interest and will have given a little preliminary thinking to the subject.

These preliminary conversations and meetings may seem to be moving slowly and your enthusiasm may prompt you to leap at once into organization, but experience has proved that group activity is not always as easy to start as it is to continue after the wheels are once in motion. Even a temporary organization gets off to a poor start unless there is a nucleus of clear-headed and purposeful poeple guiding and directing it.

THE ORGANIZATION MEETING. If your original group is agreed in the main to the plan as outlined, it is then safe to proceed with the actual organization. For this a larger group should be selected, and the invitations to the meeting should be signed by a committee of two or three at least. It is wise to allow at least a week between the issuance of the invitation and the date of the meeting.

Do not go into this organization meeting in a happy-go-lucky frame of mind, trusting that enthusiasm for the cause will bring about the desired results. Think through the meeting as you want to have it conducted, and project your imagination on into the kind of permanent organization which will grow out of it. Make mental notes of the helpful personalities and those which may not be so helpful. The bane of any public meeting is the person who talks too much and wanders far and wide away from the subject in hand. Even in a temporary organization this person must be silenced tactfully but firmly. Think over your group and try to select those who will lead in the right direction and those who will merely follow.

You may want to conduct this temporary organization meeting yourself. In that case, provide for someone else to nominate and second you as temporary chairman. Or you may not want to conduct the meeting from the chair, but to guide it as unobtrusively as possible from within the group. In that case, select your temporary chairman in advance and nominate her yourself.

Familiarize yourself, if you have not had much practical experience in parliamentary usage, with the orderly procedure in such a meeting. If your temporary organization is handled smoothly and swiftly, you have already passed the first and one of the most difficult problems and are well on your way toward permanent organization and real work.

THE TEMPORARY OFFICERS. How can a group of people organize themselves into an "assembly"? Merely by someone rising, (possibly going to the front of the room and standing by a table or desk), and saying, "I move that Mrs. Warren act as Temporary Chairman of this meeting." Someone else says, "I second the motion." The first speaker says, "All in favor of Mrs. Warren acting as Temporary Chairman will please say Aye,—those opposed No. Mrs. Warren is elected. Mrs. Warren, will you please take the chair?"

When the Temporary Chairman has been elected, she takes the chair and calls for a nomination for Temporary Secretary. When a Temporary Secretary has been nominated, seconded, and elected, she takes her place near the Temporary Chairman and keeps a record of the actions of the meeting, including the election of the Temporary Chairman and of herself. In a group of this kind, met for a common purpose, it is not advisable to nominate more than one person for each of these offices, and a single nomination and election can usually be managed without difficulty.

Your preliminary meeting has now been duly organized, with a Chairman and Secretary.

The Chairman then mentions the purpose of the meeting,—to organize a club. It is not necessary to go into details, nor to submit the question to a vote, as it may be assumed that all this has been discussed in informal conversations. The purpose of the meeting is to organize, and this should be proceeded with at once.

THE FIRST COMMITTEES. The next step is the appointment or election of committees. If the Chairman announces that the next business before the meeting is to select a Committee on Constitution and By-laws, a member may rise and say, "I move that the Chair be authorized to appoint such a committee." When this motion has been seconded and put to vote, the Chairman announces "For the Committee on Constitution and By-laws I appoint Mrs. A, Mrs. B, and Mrs. C."

A Committee on Nominations may be appointed in the same manner.

If you prefer to have these first important committees nominated by the assembly, then the Chairman may call for nominations for the Committee on Constitution and By-laws, the size of the committee having first been stipulated in advance. (Experience has taught that a small committee usually works with greater efficiency than a large one, which resembles too much an open meeting of the club itself and tends to waste time and to work at cross-purposes. For a committee of this kind it is usually sufficient to have three members, or at most five.)

Except in very large bodies nominations of this kind are made by calling out the name without rising, and it is a usual rule that no member can nominate more than one member of a committee. The Chairman repeats each name as she hears it, thus, "Mrs. Lawrence," or "Mrs. Lawrence is nominated." If no more are nominated than the number you expect to have on the committee, the Chairman assumes those mentioned to be the choice of the assembly, and announces the committee as formed. If, however, there are more nominations than there are places to be filled, the Chairman puts the questions separately on the nominations in the order in which they are made, until the required number is elected.

It is not necessary at this preliminary meeting to select more than these two committees,—one on Constitution and By-laws, and one on Nominations.

The essential preliminary work is now accomplished, and you may if you wish bring the meeting to an end at this point; or you may continue it with the idea of developing a little club spirit in the new organization. There may be a discussion of a name for the club, if one has not already been chosen. There may also be discussion of the aims of the club, with opinions from some who have not been consulted in the first conversations, but here again a word should be spoken about the danger of un-focussed and leaderless discussions. If this preliminary meeting is already so definite in its conception of the form and purpose of the proposed club that it wishes to hasten the formative period, some suggestions and advice may be given the Committee on Constitution.

The time and place for the next meeting should be fixed before the meeting breaks up.

Perhaps you will think that too much of this first meeting has been prepared in advance, that it is too "cut and dried," but this need not worry you. The group is meeting for the first time, for a single and definite purpose, and many of its members are probably unfamiliar with parliamentary practice and are timid about speaking in public. There will be plenty of opportunity for debate and the expression of divergent opinions in later meetings. For organization purposes, it is much wiser for a small group, probably not more than five or six, to agree in advance as to the Temporary Chairman and Secretary, and the personnel of the committees on Constitution and By-laws and Nominations. The necessary motions should be made and seconded promptly by a few individuals who have agreed in advance to do so.

SETTING UP A PERMANENT ORGANIZATION. At the next meeting, the Temporary Chairman calls the meeting to order and the minutes of the previous meeting are read. The report of the Committee on Constitution and By-laws is next called for. (The method by which the Constitution and By-laws are adopted is described in Chapter III.)

The Chairman then calls for the report from the Nominating Committee. As the organization is new, brought together for a common purpose, and presumably in a friendly and co-operative spirit, it is advisable for the Nominating Committee to select only one name for each office. Adoption of the report of the Nominating Committee therefore is equivalent to the election of the individuals mentioned in the report. In order to avoid any possible misunderstanding, it is wise to include this statement in the motion to accept the report of the Committee, —"Madam Chairman, I move that the report of the Nominating Committee be adopted as read and that the officers nominated be declared elected." Opportunity should be allowed for discussion after the motion has been seconded, and when the vote is taken it should be unanimous.

The permanent officers of the club have now been elected and the Temporary Chairman and Temporary Secretary retire, if their places are to be taken by others.

It is quite fitting and proper for the newly elected President to make a few informal remarks as she takes office. Some organizations have a ceremony for inducting new officers, but this is only recommended for fairly large organizations, with a taste for pomp and circumstance. For a group such as we have outlined, the less formality the better, as long as the necessary legal and parliamentary steps have been taken. For those desiring a more elaborate ritual, no set formula is provided in parliamentary procedure.

For the small cultural or working club, where the President is fairly well-known by all the members and the purposes of the club are understood and endorsed by all, the newly elected executive need not do more than express her thanks and appreciation to the members for the honor which they have conferred upon her, her earnest desire to devote herself to their leadership to the best of her ability, and her hope and confidence that she will have their good will and co-operation during her term of office. The ability to make a brief and charming speech under such circumstances is one of the most important qualifications which a presiding officer can possess. It is an ability which can be cultivated.

Having made her brief speech, the newly elected President will probably feel that her first duty is to call for adjournment. (See page 20.) Probably enough work has been accomplished for a first meeting. Possibly a social hour has been planned for, or the club may have invited a guest speaker who will discuss one of the projects for which the club has been formed, or perhaps the members of the club will have prepared a program. (In club parlance the word "program" is always used to distinguish the cultural or practical purpose of the club, as distinguished from that part of the meeting which is for the transaction of business.) If the business of the meeting is of unusual importance, involving the consideration of rather long reports or the possibility of lengthy discussion, no "program" is necessary. In that case, the call for the meeting specifically mentions the fact that it is to be a "business meeting."

PLANNING THE NEW CLUB'S FUTURE. In the interval between this first meeting of her term of office and the next meeting of the club, the President will have plenty to do. First and foremost comes the appointing of the Standing Committees. These ap-

pointments should be made at once so that the new committees
will have ample time to meet and plan their work. The Finance
Committee should prepare a budget for the first year's work.
As there is no past experience to draw from, many items in
this budget will have to be estimated or imagined, but careful
consideration of all the necessities and possibilities will arrive at
a fairly accurate total for the anticipated activities. After the
first year, the work of the Finance Committee will become
somewhat easier.

The Membership Committee gives consideration to the en-
largement of the club to the desired size and of course should
discuss frankly and freely the qualifications of any individuals
who are suggested for membership. The work of the Program
Committee should go as far as possible toward outlining a
complete and detailed program for the full year, probably ten
programs. This may not be entirely possible at this early stage,
but like the Finance Committee, the Program Committee must
use its imagination and project itself into the future as fully
as possible.

These three committees must carry the chief burden of building the framework of the new club. The other Standing Committees (mentioned in By-law V) will not have such heavy
responsibilities at the beginning, although any plans requiring
their supervision should not be overlooked.

The work of the Treasurer at this stage of development will
probably consist of setting up the books and collecting the
initiation fees and annual dues. Further work for the Treasurer
will await the adopting of a budget.

Although the new club still has no budget, a slight expenditure of money should be possible at this point. The amounts
necessary for organization are not large. Possibly they may be
advanced by a member of the club, either as a loan or as a
gift. The Recording Secretary should have a book for the

minutes, not necessarily a large leather-bound volume, but at least a book of some permanency and dignity. The Corresponding Secretary should have some paper and envelopes, with the name and address of the club printed in attractive and dignified style. A small sum should be allotted for postage. The Treasurer also needs an account book, perhaps at the beginning a simple Journal and a small Ledger will suffice. If possible, there should be neat bill forms for initiation fees and dues. Several different members of the club may make contributions to purchase these items as a donation to the club, in which case they may or may not be acknowledged by the President, and do not appear on the Treasurer's report, or they may be purchased with borrowed money, in which case they appear on the books as a debt which must be cleared in the usual way after subsequent meetings.

Once the new club is under way, the procedure is that which we have discussed fully in the opening chapters of this book.

EXAMPLE OF FORM FOR A CONSTITUTION

Article I—NAME

This club shall be called (*The Civic Club*)

Article II—PURPOSE

The purpose of this club shall be (*to study and promote civic betterment, to promote good citizenship, for study and enjoyment of the arts, etc.*)

Article III—MEMBERSHIP

The membership shall consist of (*not more than 50*) (*men or women*) (*residents of* ————.)

Article IV—OFFICERS

Section 1: The officers of this club shall be (*President, Vice-President, Secretary, Treasurer.*)

Section 2: The officers shall be elected by (*ballot*) (*at annual meeting*) (*to serve one year.*)

Article V—EXECUTIVE BOARD

Section 1: There shall be elected (*annually*) (*three members of the club to act with the officers as the Executive Board.*)

Section 2: Vacancies occurring among the officers and directors shall be filled by election by (*the Executive Board*) to serve until the next annual meeting.

Article VI—MEETINGS

Section 1: The club shall meet (*regularly*) (*on the first Monday of each month.*)

Section 2: The (*regular*) (*May*) meeting shall be the Annual

EDUCATION
FINE ARTS (Art, Music, Drama, Motion Pictures, Letters)
HOSPITALITY
HUMAN RELATIONS
INTERNATIONAL RELATIONS (World Peace)
LEGISLATIVE
MEMBERSHIP
PROGRAM
PUBLIC WELFARE
PUBLICITY
RADIO

8. The Chairman of Program should be instructed to present at the next meeting suggestions for study courses, club and community projects, which will form the basis of the Council's general program for the Club season.

9. A Council yearbook may be printed, giving the following information:

   a. Monthly meeting date: for example, the 1st Tuesday of every month.
   b. Constitution and By-laws.
   c. Officers and Chairmen, together with address and telephone number of each.
   d. Program for each meeting of the season, giving date, place, hour, name and subject of speakers, if any.

Example

PROGRAM

May 17. Elks' Hall

10:00 A.M. Business Meeting
            Committee Reports
12:30 P.M. Luncheon—Green Room
1:30 P.M.   "Our Common Cause — Democracy"
            Speaker—Mr. John Upton, Principal,
            Horton, Montana, High School

The season may be officially launched by a luncheon dedicated to "President's Day." The luncheon program in full should be given in the yearbook, also that of the annual meeting at which election of officers is held.

If the city in which a council has been organized is a large one, it may be well to divide it into districts or sections. The clubs in each district should be listed separately with information about each, also the names of the delegates and alternates to Council meetings, as follows:

FIRST DISTRICT

Shakespeare Club
Meets 1st and 3rd Wednesday
President—Mrs. Allan Port
24 Jones Avenue
Telephone: Wisconsin 7934
Delegate—Mrs. Hildreth Spoon
12 Hilldate Road
Telephone: Jericho 2135
Alternate—Mrs. Margaret Wayne
19 Fairview Road
Telephone: Spring 3487

In smaller cities, or in sections where there are not many clubs, a larger representation at Council meetings from each group will be required.

An index showing all the clubs should complete the yearbook.

NATIONAL ORGANIZATIONS FOR MEN

National Association of American Business Clubs,
Suite 401, Grier-Lincoln Hotel,
Danville, Ill.

Civitan International,
800 Farley Building,
Birmingham, Ala.

Co-operative Club International,
President Hotel,
Kansas City, Mo.

The National Exchange Club,
335 Superior Street,
Toledo, Ohio.

Gyro International,
786 Union Commerce Building,
Cleveland, Ohio.

Kiwanis International,
520 North Michigan Avenue,
Chicago, Ill.

Lions International,
350 McCormick Building,
Chicago, Ill.

National Monarch Club,
201 S. Maryland Avenue,
Elmhurst, Del.

Optimist International,
1721 Railway Exchange Building,
St. Louis, Mo.

Probus National,
1694 Main Street,
Springfield, Mass.

Rotary International,
35 East Wacker Drive,
Chicago, Ill.

Round Table International,
Shirley-Savoy Hotel,
Denver, Colo.

Ruritan National,
Windsor, Va.

The Association of 20-30 Clubs,
20-30 Building,
1915 Eye Street,
Sacramento, Cal.

Variety Clubs of America,
William Penn Hotel,
Pittsburgh, Pa.

National Association of Commonwealth Clubs,
R. A. Jackson,
Minneapolis, Minn.

The Mantle Club,
901 Orange Street,
Wilmington, Del.

International Association of Torch Clubs,
519 White Building,
Buffalo, N.Y.

NATIONAL ORGANIZATIONS FOR MEN AND WOMEN

American Farm Bureau Federation,
58 E. Washington Street,
Chicago, Ill.

Public Affairs

Public Affairs Committee,
30 Rockefeller Plaza,
New York, N.Y.

American Council on Public Affairs,
Washington, D.C.

Town Hall of the Air,
125 West 43rd Street,
New York, N.Y.

League of Women Voters,
151 East 50th Street,
New York, N.Y.

International Relations

National Council on the Cause and Cure of War,
156 Fifth Avenue,
New York, N.Y.

Foreign Policy Association,
22 East 38th Street,
New York, N.Y.

Foreign Affairs (a magazine),
45 East 65th Street,
New York, N.Y.

Pan-American Union,
Washington, D.C.

Books

National Association of Book Publishers,
347 Fifth Avenue,
New York, N.Y.

American Library Association,
520 North Michigan Avenue,
Chicago, Ill.
(Publishes a series of booklets called "Reading With a Purpose")

Music

Educational Department,
Victor Talking Machine Co.,
Camden, N.J.

Educational Department,
National Broadcasting Co.,
Rockefeller Plaza,
New York, N.Y.

National Music Week Committee,
45 West 45th Street,
New York, N.Y.

National Federation of Music Clubs,
Press-Herald Building,
Portland, Me.

Rural Life

American Farm Bureau Federation,
Chicago, Ill.

Country Gentlewoman's League,
Curtis Publishing Co.,
Independence Square,
Philadelphia, Pa.

Religion

Conference of Christians and Jews,
300 Fourth Avenue,
New York, N.Y.

The Woman's Press,
Young Women's Christian Association,
600 Lexington Avenue
New York, N.Y.

Conventions—(*Continued*)
program, 248
selection and duties of delegates, 240
Correspondence, good form, 146
necessary equipment, 142
reading of, 14
Council, local, 285

Debate, 163
control of, 73
Dues, 34
amount of, 123
delinquency, 35

Elections, methods, 103
Executive Board, 30, 39
duties of, 58

Federations, 235
(see National organizations)
Finance Committee, 40
report of, 16
Floor, obtaining the, 6
Forum, 164

Gavel, 4
Glossary of parliamentary terms, 271

Hospitality Committee, 40
House Committee, 40

Lay on the table, 66

Mail vote, 101
Majority, 94

Meetings, regular and special, 32
Members, election of, 33
responsibilities of, 2, 8
Membership, committee, 40
size and classification, 29
Membership Committee, 40
report of, 16
Men's and women's clubs, 238, 270, 290
Men's clubs, customs, 262
hobby clubs, 267
lunch or dinner clubs, 263
programs of dinner clubs, 265
public affairs, 268
service clubs, 268
Minutes, essentials, 88
example, 90
necessary materials, 84
of committee meetings, 87
reading of, 13
what to include and omit, 86
when signed, 88
Money-raising, 126
Motions, amendable, 62
debatable, 62
how to amend, 71
how to dispose of, 66
(see summary, 277)
how to make, 60
how to second, 61
incidental, 69
main, 62
out of order, 74
privileged, 67
secondary, 64

subsidiary, 64
wording of, 24

National organizations, 235, 290
for men, 237, 288
for men and women, 238, 270, 290
for women, 236, 287
New business, 19
New clubs, first committees, 229
how to organize, 224
organization meeting, 227
temporary officers, 228
Nominating Committee, 40, 108
Nomination, committee, 108
floor, 105
methods of, 104
rotation, 111

Officers, duties of, 30, 37, 46
election of, 30
Order of business, 11, 41
Orders of the day, 68
Out of order, 74

Panel, 164
Papers, 169
collecting material, 173
essentials of presentation, 184
federal publications, 177
how to use material, 178
influence of radio, 170
libraries, 175
magazines and newspapers, 174
membership participation, 171

Parliamentarian, 22
Parliamentary authority, 43
Parliamentary law, glossary, 271
proper use of, 22
purpose of, 1, 8,
summary of, 277
Parliamentary terms, glossary, 271
Plurality, 93
Postpone, 65
President, 37
correspondence, 145
duties of, 48
Presiding officer, 25
when may vote, 102
Previous question, 66
Program Committee, 40
correspondence, 145
meeting the out of town guest, 159
powers and responsibilities, 151
selecting speakers, 172
selection of, 150
Programs, budget, 158
methods of discussion, 162
participation of members, 161
radio, 165
speakers, 155
subjects for, 153
year book, 166
Proxy, 101
Public speaking, 186
before the audience, 192
how to practice, 189

Publicity, co-operation of members and officers, 209
  how to prepare copy, 207
  use of pictures, 206
  value of, 200
  work of chairman, 201

Quorum, 12, 41

Receipts, 117
Recognition, how to obtain, 6
Resolutions, form of, 76
  importance of, 82
  publicity for, 83
  safeguarding, 81
  types of, 75
Resolutions Committee, 40
  duties of, 77, 79
Reviving an old club, 222
Rise, when to, 5, 23
Rising vote, 97
Roll-call, 12
  voting by, 98

Secretary, Corresponding, 38
  duties of, 56, 144
  necessary equipment, 142
Secretary, Recording, 37
  duties of, 54
Seminar, 165
Service club, American citizenship, 211
  choosing activities, 211
  community improvement, 215
  education, 217
  international relations, 218

libraries, 213
  student loan-funds, 216
  the arts, 218
Show of hands, 97
Speakers, 155
Special Committees, 18, 133
Special funds, 119
Study, sources of information,
  290
Symposium, 165

Treasurer, 38
  audit, 119
  bank account, 117
  bills and receipts, 117
  correct signature, 119
  correspondence, 145
  duties of, 57, 114
  legal receipt, 119
  necessary equipment, 115
  report of, 15, 118
  special funds, 119
Two-thirds vote, 94

Unfinished business, 19

Vice-President, 37
  duties of, 53
Viva voce, 96
Voting, methods of, 24, 93, 95
  terms used, 93
Women's clubs, community activities, 257
  customs and etiquette, 257
  social element, 259

Year book, 166

subsidiary, 64
wording of, 24

National organizations, 235, 290
    for men, 237, 288
    for men and women, 238, 270, 290
    for women, 236, 287
New business, 19
New clubs, first committees, 229
    how to organize, 224
    organization meeting, 227
    temporary officers, 228
Nominating Committee, 40, 108
Nomination, committee, 108
    floor, 105
    methods of, 104
    rotation, 111

Officers, duties of, 30, 37, 46
    election of, 30
Order of business, 11, 41
Orders of the day, 68
Out of order, 74

Panel, 164
Papers, 169
    collecting material, 173
    essentials of presentation, 184
    federal publications, 177
    how to use material, 178
    influence of radio, 170
    libraries, 175
    magazines and newspapers, 174
    membership participation, 171

Parliamentarian, 22
Parliamentary authority, 43
Parliamentary law, glossary, 271
    proper use of, 22
    purpose of, 1, 8,
    summary of, 277
Parliamentary terms, glossary, 271
Plurality, 93
Postpone, 65
President, 37
    correspondence, 145
    duties of, 48
Presiding officer, 25
    when may vote, 102
Previous question, 66
Program Committee, 40
    correspondence, 145
    meeting the out of town guest, 159
    powers and responsibilities, 151
    selecting speakers, 172
    selection of, 150
Programs, budget, 158
    methods of discussion, 162
    participation of members, 161
    radio, 165
    speakers, 155
    subjects for, 153
    year book, 166
Proxy, 101
Public speaking, 186
    before the audience, 192
    how to practice, 189